SERMONS

ON THE

CHRISTIAN LIFE.

BY THE

RIGHT REV. GEORGE BURGESS, D. D.,

Bishop of the Protestant Episcopal Church in the Diocese of Maine.

PHILADELPHIA:
PUBLISHED BY HERMAN HOOKER,
S. W. COR. CHESTNUT AND EIGHTH STREETS.
STANFORD & SWORDS, NEW YORK:
IDE & DUTTON, BOSTON.
1854.

PRINTED BY ISAAC ASHMEAD.

CONTENTS.

SERMON IX.

SERMON X.

SERMON XI.

SERMON XII.

SERMON XIII.

SERMON XIV.

SERMON XV.

SERMON XVI.

SERMON XVII.

SERMON XVIII.

SERMON XIX.

PREFACE.

THE publisher of this volume has been anxiously desirous to promote, by such means as his position might place in his power, the habit of reading for direct religious edification. He has believed that, both in the private chamber and in the family circle, especially when any are deprived, wholly or partially, of the privileges of the sanctuary, no other books will quite supply the place of printed sermons; and he has regretted that, in our country, so few volumes of this class are offered to the public. In the hope that the taste of thoughtful persons may not be yet at settled variance with what was formerly esteemed so favourable to the growth of individual and domestic piety, he determined to enter on the publication of several volumes from living preachers of the Church, if their consent could be obtained, and if the first results of the enterprise should not be mere discouragements. Under these motives, application was made to the author of the present volume, for a selection of simple, practical sermons, from the ordinary course of his parochial instructions.

This request is the sole cause of the appearance of the following Discourses. Having prepared and preached them, as he hoped, with the testimony of a good conscience, the writer could have no dread of giving them a more permanent form or a wider publicity, except that which might spring from solicitude for his literary reputation. In his judgment, such an apprehension ought not to be permitted to utter itself, when a Christian brother desired only to employ them for purposes of direct usefulness, and urgently claimed the whole responsibility. They are therefore printed, with almost as little hesitation as would have preceded the compliance with a request to preach them again; and with no other wish or fear or anxiety than those with which every true minister of our Lord Jesus Christ, within our communion, kneels down every Sunday in his pulpit, before he opens his lips to speak, a sinner to sinners, of the way to life eternal.

SERMON I.

NO MAN LIVETH TO HIMSELF.

Romans, xiv. 7.

"For none of us liveth to himself."

This grand, broad principle is applied by St. Paul to Christians. They are not their own, but are the servants of that Lord who has redeemed them and has made them brethren. They live to the Lord; and then, for his sake, and in obedience to his injunction, and to that renewed nature which they have received from him, and which is formed after his image, they live also to one another. To him they must render their account; to him they must stand or fall; and they are not to judge one another, but with charitable forbearance to seek that no man put a stumbling-block or an occasion of falling, in the way of any fellow Christian. All the members have not the same office; but all may make increase of the body unto the edifying of itself in love.

The very same principle must be applied, not merely to good men as they stand together in the Church, but to good men as they stand together in all society: for God is the author of the institution of society, as well as of that communion which unites his people. He has made men to live together; he has joined them in the relations of the family and the state; he has appointed that business and toil, in their various forms, should be duties and necessities. We cannot dwell alone; and his Church cannot, if it would, go away and sojourn apart from the residue of mankind. So far as religion rules, it makes society itself a Christian body; and certainly, the same principles and feelings which determine how one Christian should stand towards another, must be the basis of the relations between man and his fellow-men, as these were originally intended and instituted by Him who made all things good.

This explanation was desirable: because the light in which it is now designed to consider the principle declared in the text, is that in which it appears as placed at the foundation of all society; as a rule of all social action; and especially as binding together our religious life and the business, as we term it, of the world.

If you imagine a number of persons thrown

upon an island where they were thenceforth to live, severed by the ocean from all other countries, you perceive at once that no one of them would live for himself; that at least no one could live long for himself only. They must divide their toils, so that each one should perform some particular office for the rest. Some must till the ground; some must construct boats; some must be fishers on the sea; some must remain at home to prepare food. Here is a very simple example; and it is evident that out of these several employments would grow up, in a short time, the whole texture of our social arrangements, with all their division of labour. When any one should appear to possess a special skill in one branch of toil, the others would have recourse to his services in that department. If any one were specially disqualified for certain tasks, those tasks would be left to others, and he would be assigned to those to which he might be deemed equal. He who had bodily strength would labor vigorously with his hands. He whose mind was fitted for the work of instruction might become a teacher. If any one had experience in the treatment of diseases, he would be summoned to administer to the sick. If disputes arose, some wiser than the rest would soon be appointed by the general voice to sit as judges and magistrates. In the mean time, such as might be afflicted with sickness, or weighed down by age, or visited with any accidental disability, would receive from the labors of the rest a due provision for their sustenance and comfort. But if any one would live in sloth, he would naturally be left to suffer some inconvenience for his refusal to assist the common cause, as well as to provide for himself; and if any one would withdraw himself, and attempt to provide for himself alone, neither asking nor giving, neither borrowing nor lending, he would be compelled to pay the penalty of his selfishness in a miserable destitution of all social comforts and of many personal enjoyments, which might otherwise have been easily and cheaply purchased.

Should such a community, in process of time, become a numerous state, the mutual connection of the members would only be the more widely extended, and the more complete. The same principle would still preside. Necessity, which is nothing else but the will of God in his providence, makes men subservient to the wants of each other, whether they constitute merely a family, or a city, or a colony, or a nation. Even different nations become linked together into one vast system by foreign commerce. Each has its own productions, its own materials for manufactures, its own peculiar talents and facilities. God gives them the world and all which it contains, in joint dominion; and they are so to divide its fruits amongst themselves, and so to employ all the powers with which they are entrusted, that each may be partaker of the benefit, and that the greatest good of all may be the result of the whole system.

This we must all perceive to be the construction of human society. It is so arranged that even the wrath of men shall in some sense serve God; that his good purposes shall be fulfilled even by those who despise his laws, and who intend to live, and suppose that they are living, only to themselves. They are selfishly seeking, each one only to improve his own condition, and to add to his own gains; but they cannot avoid contributing at the same time to the common good. So, nations are fed and clothed, and furnished with the arts and luxuries of every climate; and the world, under the government of its divine Sovereign, is proceeding towards a riper civilization and a completer happiness. It is impossible that we should not bear a part in the accomplishment of his supreme purposes; but to bear a noble, a willing, an active, a conscious part, is the duty to which we are called; and it will have its blessed recompense.

From this view of society, it follows that every one of us occupies in it a place which has been assigned him for the general good by the overruling Providence. "Let every man," says the Apostle elsewhere, "abide in the calling wherein he is called," so that the believer is required to regard himself as thus under an injunction to remain at his place and in it to fulfil his Christian duty. This is the first suggestion which proceeds from our consideration of this established order. A man is where he is, because he has been placed there by a higher appointment. It is not through any mere accident, nor through any mere choice of his own, apart from the will of his Maker. This world, fallen as it is, and in bondage, has never been torn from the supreme control of God; and the wisdom which measures out our lives, and endues us with our faculties, prepares us also for our stations, and fixes us in these stations. How little have most of us done to determine our own education, opportunities and employments! Our particular trade or profession we may have chosen with some freedom; but we have been so placed, without our care, that we could not but choose amongst a few, and within a certain class of avocations. It could not have been far otherwise than it is; and we are satisfied as we look back that our steps were ordered. A great thing it is, too, that any one shall have this feeling. It lifts him and his calling up at once into a higher region, and clothes him at once with a conscious dignity, confidence and responsibility. If his lot should be what in the world is deemed a more humble one, he will entertain no humiliating sentiment; for no place is mean, which God has assigned. Just as little can he perceive any ground for pride, if his position be more elevated in the esteem of men: it is but the gift of God, with its appropriate trust. Are your occupations such as afford you the constant gratification of your taste, and yield many enjoyments as you pass along? They may continually remind you of the goodness which has caused the lines to fall for you in pleasant places, and which thus leads you to repentance by the bonds of love. Is your way one of much hardship, difficulty and annoyance? It is still the way which you have been enjoined to tread, and in which you are constantly doing the service which has been laid upon you by the great heavenly Taskmaster. You are not, in any event, living to yourself, but to God and your fellow-men; since such is the ordinance of Him who gave you life and breath and being.

Where we do in any measure select our own sphere of life, this very thought should constrain us not to seek simply our own pleasure. There are modes of employment and of gain which, though they are within the dominion of God, are by no means of his institution. To undertake a demoralizing business because it is profitable, is to cut off the daily employment of life from the divine design. He who does this cannot live to himself, though he desires it; for, while he injures others by his occupation, he lays up a double wrath against the day of wrath, and can never be judged as if he had wronged his own soul only. It was not meant that any demoralizing business should exist in society; it is not needed by society; and he who follows it would live to himself if it were in his power, but must suffer with his victims. What more utter baseness can be imagined than that of encouraging others to vice, for the sake of making a profit from their iniquities? They who will deliberately engage in occupations which they know to be maintained by wickedness, and to nourish wickedness, must give their awful account to him who has ordained that each should live not for the ruin, but for the advantage of the whole body of which he is a member. Content to enrich themselves through the sins of others, they are doing what cannot be undone; and the day will come when they would throw all their gains into the sea to buy a clean conscience. But in the choice of occupations, there should be something more than merely to avoid such guilt; guilt which it is so much easier to avoid at first, than afterwards to break off and relinquish. Almost all kinds of business are directly useful to society, and the mode of their usefulness appears at the first glance. All agriculture, all commerce, all mechanical and manufacturing employments, are simply useful in supplying the necessities and administering to the comfort of mankind. The farm furnishes the food of all. The ships transport the produce of the earth, and of human toil. It is moulded and formed for its various uses in a thousand manufactories. It is collected and sold in the shop of the tradesman, and the warehouse of the merchant. Millions are busy every where in preparing for other millions food, clothing, shelter, warmth, light, conveniences of every kind, and all which adorns the dwellings of men. Every one of these millions, husbandman, mariner, merchant, mechanic, laborer, whatever be his particular calling, is passing his days in occupations which pour something into the general stock and treasury of comforts. One class of persons transport the traveller on his way; another class provide him, wherever he arrives, a temporary home. They do for a payment, what, if it could not be so done, or could not be paid for, would be the utmost exercise of kindness and hospitality; and it is not the less for the good of the traveller, because he is able and expects to render a remuneration. Advance farther; and what clearer benefit can be conferred than that education, which is the business of the schoolmaster? Or, what is more necessary than that defence for which the magistrate and the soldier bear the sword? Or, what is more important to the safety of each individual than the offices of the judge, the advocate, and all the administrators of the laws? Or, who comes with an earthly blessing so precious as that which is brought by him who can become, under God, the restorer of health? I will not speak of those whose happy duty it is to preach the unsearchable riches of Christ, and to offer that pearl of great price which would be cheaply purchased with the loss of all wealth beside. A person can hardly select and pursue any calling amongst the multitude of ordinary callings, without being useful. Happy for all of us that such are the vast majority of stations and occupations in all Christian countries. With all these before him, how wretched must be the choice of him who opens a play-house, or a gambling-house, or a drinking-house; or who cheats the public by introducing some false article into traffic and use; or who writes, publishes or sells such books and sheets as corrupt the mind and heart! But let us go much farther. The mass of occupations are directly useful, as well as not injurious; and although there are some which, without having much real utility of their own, are so wrought into the general system that they cannot well be separated, yet a good man would prefer to feel that what he is daily forming or obtaining with his hand is something which really assists the general welfare and happiness. Such a man, I think, would prefer to sell or to prepare food, clothing, or medicine, rather than implements of destruction, even though these may sometimes be lawfully employed, under a stern necessity. To dig gold is useful; for gold is needed for coinage and for ornament. But he who digs iron or coal, or who digs in a field of vegetables, or on a railroad embankment, may feel himself to be more directly useful, and may more respect his calling. However this may be, let those who can choose their occupation, choose one in which they can hope to do some obvious good; and they will always be the happier, even though they should be the less wealthy.

Much more important, however, is it that all should be exhorted in the constant exercise of their callings, to remember always that they are not living to themselves. Let their motives be such as this truth should suggest; for the motive can make the most useful occupation useless to him by whom it is pursued; and that which promises least, can, through the motive, become a crown of glory. Under this consciousness, how easy is it to be contented! The most common tasks of business become labors of love, when we know that they are appointed us by God, as our part in the providential maintenance of society with all its blessings. A different spirit is thus breathed into every transaction. Business is no longer followed, as if all labor were a mere slavish drudgery; nor yet merely for filthy lucre's sake; nor yet in any mere selfishness; nor yet with the thorough devotion of the whole soul, as if we had no other labor but that of business. It becomes a field for the exercise of Christian sincerity, faithfulness and diligence. Whatever is to be done, is to be done in the best manner. Those opportunities of performing acts of kindness and beneficence, which are interspersed amidst the business of every life are now welcomed, and find the heart ready. Over all reigns the delightful consciousness that life is not thrown away, that it is a sacrifice, reasonable, holy and living, presented to the Giver of every good gift, and used by Him for his honor.

It is a happy effect of this view that it tends to break down that too high and strong distinction which is sometimes made between the business of the world and that of religion. They are often represented as directly opposite, and as almost irreconcilable. It then appears as if one must be laid by before the other is begun. This is a great and mischievous delusion, for it makes the Christian worldly as well as timid, and it makes the worldly man worldlier. The former fears to use the world as not abusing it, and is tempted to do like those who doubt and yet eat, and so sin against their conscience; the latter abuses the world, deliberately and boldly. Both feel the necessity of living and laboring in the world; and both are aware that men cannot be thorough in their business without throwing into it something of their hearts. It is so; and neither need the Christian withdraw from all interest in the business of the world, nor can the worldly man be excused for casting himself headlong into that business, with the intention to forget God and live to himself. But no man liveth to himself, and no man ought to wish it; and he who desires to serve God and do good, may be assured that he fulfils his desire when in the fear of God he does well the duty of his station and calling. Could this unnatural distinction between business and practical religion be removed, so that the former should be seen to be comprehended within the latter, it might be hoped that some who now hold themselves aloof from religion and its interests, might learn the better way. You are not to forsake your work, your trade, your office or profession, nor to follow it with indifference. Let it concern you as before, but not selfishly; nor as the mere means of making you richer; nor as a burden which must be endured for the sake of a living. It is your work and duty; your part in the great social system, of which God, and not man, has originally laid the foundations, and distributed the several portions. Do it as well as you can, and as successfully as you may be permitted; and give it so much of your thoughts and heart as, in your conscientious judgment, it demands and deserves, in comparison with other duties. But there is a great first duty with which no necessary business can ever interfere. It is to believe in Christ; to seek peace with God through the one Mediator and Redeemer; and to give up your souls and your lives to his service. Do this, and then, with the strength which you shall draw from your faith, go to your business and to all the duties of your daily occupations. They will then be easy, pleasant and noble in your sight; and you will find in them aids to your own salvation, and means of constant glory to God and good to your generation.

"No man liveth to himself." But men do live without acknowledging any higher law than their own desires, or obeying any better motive than their own natural feelings and passions, or seeking any purer end than their own gratification. Let conscience say, my brother, whether it is thus with you. If it be thus, all is wrong; and you must indeed be renewed in the spirit of your mind before you can enjoy a true and reliable hope of heaven. "He that is faithful in that which is least, is faithful also in much;" and if the Lord is not now your Lord, there would be no heart for his service in a higher state hereafter. If you do not desire to do his will while you dwell here, how could you obey him, as citizens of the Jerusalem which is above? The idolatry of self would banish you thence, and shut you out from all joy; for, in the whole creation, there is no place of rest for creatures like us, till we have learned to live to God and to our brethren. "He that loveth, dwelleth in God, and God in him."

SERMON II.

THE WHOLE ARMOUR OF GOD.

Ephesians, vi. 13.

"WHEREFORE, TAKE UNTO YOU THE WHOLE ARMOUR OF GOD, THAT YE MAY BE ABLE TO WITHSTAND IN THE EVIL DAY, AND, HAVING DONE ALL, TO STAND."

A GENTLE flock, feeding in green pastures; ranging along the banks of still waters; following the voice of a kind shepherd; and either safe within the fold, or equally safe abroad, because he is near, furnishes a delightful image of peace. An exposed army, encompassed by enemies; taking, each man to himself, every weapon or piece of armour, offensive or defensive; all on their guard against assault, and not the less watchful against stratagem, is a stirring image of danger. It seems impossible that both should represent the same persons in the same state; and yet, both are equally employed in Scripture, and, we are sure, with equal truth, to represent the company of Christian believers in that state to which they are called by their profession.

Not by images alone, but also in the most direct and plainest language, has Christ declared that the condition of his people is a condition of peace, and at the same time a condition of war. "Peace, I leave with you," was his parting word; "peace be unto you; "these things have I spoken unto you, that in me ye might have peace." But at other times he said, "Suppose ye, that I am come to send peace upon earth? I come not to send peace, but a sword." "Ye shall be hated of all men for my name's sake." "He that hath no sword, let him sell his garment, and buy one."

The contrast, broad though it be, contains no real difficulty. No man who ever entered on a Christian life could avoid understanding, from his own experience, that it has both these sides; that it is a state both of the happiest peace and of the deadliest conflict. Without, all may be strife, while all within is sunshine. The people of God may be hated by the world, while they have sweet peace amongst themselves. There may even be contention between them, and yet peace in the conscience even of those who, through mistake or frailty or necessity, are still contending. Within the mind itself there is a war, and a peace; a peace, more or less conscious and sure, through the blood of Jesus and the grace of the Holy Ghost; a war against all remaining sin, a war not to cease till we are where the wicked cease from troubling, and the weary are at rest. One chain of peace and love binds together all the followers of the Lamb in one communion of the saints, and binds them in that communion to the blessed above, and to the Lord of all. But so much the more are they at war, at wrestling, irreconcilable war, "with principalities and powers, with the rulers of the darkness of this world, with spiritual wickedness in high places;" with Satan and all his hosts, all his devices, all his instruments. This is the war of which in the text, the apostle has spoken; and let us now, in dependence on the gracious teaching of the Holy Spirit, consider the *enemies*, the *conflict*, the *armour*, and the *result*.

The *enemies* are real, formidable, subtle and mighty. It is difficult to comprehend the agency of the powers of darkness. It is difficult to comprehend any spiritual agency. But no hour can pass without affording its evidence, that our minds are subject to temptation. The origin of the sins which take such possession of innumerable minds, is as clear as the origin and progress of any thought, action, habit or mode of living. Temptation is the source of sins, and sin is the flood which leaves misery all along its banks. Our own judgment and the uniform language of the Scriptures thus trace back all earthly wickedness and woe to those temptations which spring at first from the invisible operation of "the spirit that now worketh in the children of disobedience," "the prince of this world," "the devil, who is a murderer from the beginning, a liar and the father of lies." Let us go no further on this awful ground; but let us be assured, that the enemy by whose temptations the first Adam fell, and whose temptations, one after another, the second Adam overcome by the word of God, is as real as our own spirits and our own iniquities. These iniquities are his work; and thus they become his instruments, and our enemies.

Our enemies are formidable; for see, what multitudes are led away captive! The Scriptures designate the world itself as lying in sin, and as the dominion, in a certain sense, of the evil one; not as if it were wrested from the hand of its Maker; not as if it were all evil; but they indicate thus how extensive has become the control of sin over the hearts of men; and they place this world in contrast with those more glorious regions of the universe, in which sin and sorrow are unknown. We live on this enchanted ground, as it were, where temptation is never very far off; where our adversary goeth about as a roaring lion, seeking whom he may devour. And if we fail at last, oh, who can bear to think of the soul that falls into the hands of such enemies, and is doomed to their society!

Those enemies are subtle; for Satan can appear as an angel of light, and our own hearts are deceitful. Were it otherwise, the task of resistance would be simple; but never, since that forbidden fruit was presented, which was pleasant to the eye, and good for food, and seemed to be desirable to make one wise, never has sin lacked an amiable or attractive disguise. The subtlety of our enemies is exercised in covering the blackness and depravity of guilt; in making evil appear good, and good evil; in hiding great sins under the form of their small beginnings; in seducing to the first step, which to the eye is comparatively slight, but from which the second and the third are so much easier; in perverting the word of God, so as to create prejudice against the truth, and to persuade men to deny it in their hearts, while they appear to themselves only to give it a peculiar interpretation; and in sowing, under every pretence, the seeds of discord, hatred and uncharitableness, so that men view themselves as champions for right, while they are but struggling to gratify their own will or passions. That man knows less than half of his own danger, who is only on his guard against the *open* assaults of sin. It is to be so far suspected every where that we should walk like soldiers in a savage land, who know that the next moment they may be assailed by a host in ambush.

Looking onward, too, rather than within, we may well say that these enemies are mighty. Think what a fortress, when the apostle wrote, was before the few and humble followers of the gospel. Princes and empires, temples and priests and worshippers, all the institutions and customs of human society, were in subjection to these falsehoods which were to be overthrown. The whole vast system of idolatry was to be leveled with the ground. A simple, holy religion was to take its place upon the ruins of all that mass of vices which the heathen superstitions allowed and almost seemed to consecrate. Every evil propensity of the human heart, every lust of the flesh, all that gratifies pride, ambition, the love of money, or the thirst for pleasure, was in arms against the doctrine of Christ crucified. Against all these the apostles wrestled;

and against them all we are called to wrestle still, so far as they still prevail. How much do they indeed prevail, all except the worship of idols of wood and stone, which has so long since yielded, but to which, even in our own times, and in a seemingly Christian shape, some are ready to return! There is no wickedness, no misery, no form of evil, against which we are not, as Christians, enlisted. The cause of God is hostile to them all. Our Saviour came to take them away. While he was here upon earth, he went about doing good, and, as a mighty conqueror, rescuing the captives of sin, redeeming the victims of sorrow, and at length subduing the dominion of death. In the same cause, we take his service under his banners. Sin within us, and sin around us; Satan, as the author of sin, and misery as the consequence of sin; these are our enemies; alas, how mighty every where!

The *conflict* requires little explanation; for in resisting sin by every possible means, we accomplish all that we have undertaken. Sin is to be renounced from the first; it is to be opposed, where opposition is in our power; it is to be bewailed, where we can do no more. The conflict is one, however, in which there can be no truce, no pause, no compromise. Nothing else is to be hated; all animosity is to be concentrated against that one foe of foes. But the conflict embraces many scenes, and it is to be conducted in every manner which the human powers allow, and which the word of God approves. There are wars in which certain means only are employed, or certain territories only are contested; wars, in which the victor intends to stay his hand after certain successes, and the vanquished have only to fear a certain degree of danger or humiliation. It is not so with this struggle; all is at hazard, and wherever sin raises its head, the Christian combatant is bound to fight manfully, till he can tread it down. We may well say, too, that all means are profitable and commendable, because against sin every thing may be tried except what is sinful; and to use sin against sin would be no conflict. The word of God approves all which is not wrong in this warfare; and what is wrong would be, not resistance, but submission. Our business is simply, to withstand in the evil day; and the evil day is always, when sin is at hand.

But the chief subject suggested by the text and the succeeding words, is rather the *armour*, the weapons with which this conflict is to be carried on. "Take unto you the whole armour of God." The apostle proceeds to enumerate the several pieces of this suit of holy armour. "Stand, therefore, having your loins girt about with truth;" for truth is here compared with the girdle, which, surrounding the body, gave compactness to the whole attire and armour, and enabled the champion to act with promptness, and with the free, unembarrassed exercise of all his energies. It seems to be rather truth of heart than truth in doctrine; but the one is the companion of the other; for truth of heart leads to truth of doctrine; and truth of doctrine would be of little value without truth of heart. He who possesses a godly sincerity towards God and man, has no motive for disguising from himself the truth as it is in Jesus. Because he is true, he seeks, he loves, he holds, he speaks that truth; and the consciousness of such sincerity gives to the Christian what the girdle gave to the ancient warriors. He is not fettered in his movements: his weapons are ready; his garments hang closely, yet easily around him. This it is to be conscious of truth; to have no other purposes to serve than those of truth; to feel ourselves sure and steadfast in the truth, not driven to and fro by a doubting and uncertain mind, nor yet ever suspicious of the cause we are defending. Let your loins be girt about with truth; and you stand erect, firm, ready for diligent action.

Beneath this girdle of truth, the Christian warrior is to have on the breastplate of righteousness. It is what St. Paul elsewhere terms "the armour of righteousness on the right hand and on the left." It is righteousness of intent: it is righteousness of conduct. A familiar sentiment is expressed in the line,

"Thrice is he armed, who has his quarrel just."

That expression indicates the temper and spirit in which a man can act, who is doing, and knows that he is doing, righteousness towards his fellow-men, and striving thus also to keep a good conscience towards God. Without it, the Christian must ever be exposed to all his enemies on every side. Men will see his sin, and make it his reproach. The Evil One will exult over him, as already all but a captive. Every deed of unrighteousness, every act known to be wrong is a breach in this breastplate; and if they are but multiplied, they soon leave us quite defenceless. Nay, if even a few, or any, be deliberately permitted, and remain unrepented, the subtle adversary will find that spot, and there aim his deadly blow. Oh, how impossible it is to prize too highly the safety which is afforded to the Christian, as he walks amidst enemies, by a blameless and a righteous conduct in every relation and duty!

Next, the feet must be "shod with the preparation of the gospel of peace." The legs and feet of the ancient warrior were not left undefended; for they had much to perform in the attack, the struggle, the pursuit, and, if need were, the flight and escape. But as our feet are to be swift, not to shed blood, but to do good, our appropriate greaves or sandals are "the preparation of the gospel of peace;" and it may be that the apostle alludes to that exclamation of the prophet; "how beautiful upon the mountains are the feet of them that preach the gospel of peace, and bring glad tidings of good things!" So, not only the ministers of that gospel, but every believer should make haste to bring these tidings, and with them all righteousness, peace and joy in the Holy Ghost.

Over all the shield of faith is to be suspended, "wherewith ye shall be able to quench all the fiery darts of the wicked." The shield was the great instrument of defence; because, held by an active hand under a watchful eye, it not only guarded the vital parts, but it could be turned in every direction from which danger might proceed, and could dash back every assailing weapon· Such is faith to the Christian. Around him fly the fiery darts of wicked spirits, and of wicked men; every kind of temptation to which his sinful nature offers a mark. But if they find him armed with the impenetrable shield of a faith which remains unshaken, a faith which is the substance of things hoped for; if to all which temptation can promise, faith can oppose a promise of that which is far, far better; and to all which temptation can threaten, a danger which is far, far more terrible, and to every suggestion the simple reply, "thus it is written in the word of God, and thus I believe;" the darts will fall without harm; their fiery, envenomed points will be quenched or blunted; and faith will make temptation powerless. How striking, how real, is this scriptural imagery! The wicked, the wicked One, as the original may seem to signify, sends his thick shower of blazing arrows, which carry a twofold death by their points and by their flames; but in the midst of them all the Christian soldier presses steadily on; and, as they lie, deprived of all their mischief by the shield of his strong faith, he treads them all in the dust.

Still more: he wears "the helmet of salvation." The exact significance of this expression must be learned from a corresponding one in the first epistle to the Thessalonians. There, the apostle speaks of "putting on the breastplate of faith and love," as here of the breastplate of righteousness and the shield of faith, "and for an helmet the hope of salvation." In this life, salvation is ours chiefly in hope; and this is here compared with the helmet. For the helmet crowned all the rest of the armour, and was adorned with the crest and floating plume. It seemed to express the glory of the war, and the confidence of expected triumph; and at the same time it was strong, and defended one of the great seats of life. This is the province of Christian hope, of salvation possessed in hope. It cheers; it adorns; it animates; it strengthens. He who hopes much is prepared to lead; others are warmed by his example; and his very hope of life eternal, saves him against a thousand of those poor temptations which worldly hopes present, as well as against the crushing onset of terror and despair.

All these are defensive weapons: the one weapon of offence, which the Christian is to wield, is "the sword of the Spirit, which is the word of God." The armour with which we are to defend ourselves, is the gift of divine grace; but once given us, it may be worn as our own. These weapons of defence are what God has created within us. The sole weapon of offence is not only given by him, but given as still his own, and only capable of being taken up by us, and wielded in his strength and in his service. "Quick and powerful" is that word, and "sharper than any two-edged sword, piercing even to the dividing asunder of the joints and marrow." With this we do much more than guard ourselves: we push the war against principalities and powers; we assail the hosts of darkness; and we prevail, because it is in the hearts alone of men that the empire of Satan is to be dreaded, and the word of God, enforced by the Spirit, whose sword it is, goes straight home to the heart. There, it must inflict the wound which itself alone can heal; convincing the conscience, enlightening the inward eyes, subduing all imaginations, and bringing every thought into captivity to the obedience of Christ. Thus the Redeemer triumphs over many souls; thus must he yet triumph throughout the world.

Soldiers of Christ, behold your armour, and put it on. God gives it freely; "ask, and ye shall receive." Then, go in armour to the conflict; you, who have long been serving in this war, and you who are just ready to avow your enlistment. The *result* cannot be doubtful. When the men of New England, a century ago, were about to attempt an immense warlike enterprise for the security of their homes, the counsel and prayers of the pious Whitefield were sought by some of their commanders. He gave them, as a motto for their flags, words which were a consecration of a passage in a Roman poet; and which, thus varied from their original application by introducing the name of the Captain of our salvation, might be translated,

"Where Christ thy leader leads, despair of naught."

Those flags, through the striking favor of Providence, soon waved over the strong and distant fortress of their adversaries. In such a spirit, fight the good fight of faith. Be but sure that you steadfastly follow Christ; and then you are sure of being conquerors, and more than conquerors. You shall withstand with success in the evil day; and, having done all, you shall stand, in that great, glorious day, when he shall have put all enemies under his feet; all his enemies, and yours.

SERMON III.

GROSS SINS.

Ephesians, chap. iv. 25—29.

"WHEREFORE, PUTTING AWAY LYING, SPEAK EVERY MAN TRUTH WITH HIS NEIGHBOR: FOR WE ARE MEMBERS ONE OF ANOTHER. BE YE ANGRY, AND SIN NOT; LET NOT THE SUN GO DOWN UPON YOUR WRATH; NEITHER GIVE PLACE TO THE DEVIL. LET HIM THAT STOLE, STEAL NO MORE; BUT RATHER LET HIM LABOR, WORKING WITH HIS HANDS THE THING WHICH IS GOOD, THAT HE MAY HAVE TO GIVE TO HIM THAT NEEDETH. LET NO CORRUPT COMMUNICATION PROCEED OUT OF YOUR MOUTH, BUT THAT WHICH IS GOOD TO THE USE OF EDIFYING, THAT IT MAY MINISTER GRACE UNTO THE HEARERS."

IN discourses addressed to a congregation assembled in the house of God, it is very common to suppose that those to whom they are addressed, already possess a certain elevation and pureness of moral principle. Often, it seems to be presumed, that even of the less devout amongst them, each one resembles the young man to whom our Saviour said, "one thing thou lackest." It is, indeed, quite fair to presume that the worst portion of society are not collected in places of public worship. But it by no means follows that all who are there are free from even the grosser vices; much less, that they can never be brought into gross temptation. St. Paul, in the text, admonishes the members of a Christian Church to abstain from lying and stealing, from wrathful contention, and from corrupt communication; and the nature of man must be greatly changed before similar exhortations can be deemed wholly unsuitable in any mingled assembly. The barrier between common propriety of conduct and vice is not so high, that it may not be overleaped; nor can any man who nourishes in his heart an evil root, determine to what stature the plant shall grow. They who have not the security of God's grace, may at any time be far nearer than they are aware to some act of startling criminality; and they who have that security, retain it only by watchfulness and prayer.

How often has a community been smitten with horror at the disclosure of appalling guilt, where suspicion had never approached! How often have family circles, the most respected, and even the most eminent, been overwhelmed by the tidings that one of their members has proved a thief, or a forger, or an adulterer, or even a murderer! How often have young persons grown up in the bosom of all which is most refined and refining, to bring all the dishonor of crime on themselves and on their kindred! How often may the Christian pastor reflect, with bitter pain and with trembling, that if a very slight line were passed by some amongst the younger of his charge, they might proceed at once from profane levity and recklessness into unprincipled excess and daring guilt! It is well that a deep horror of crime should be enforced by precept upon precept; that so, seeing the terrible end of the path, many may be deterred from its entrance; or if they have entered it, may be persuaded to forsake it while yet they can, without waiting even for to-morrow. Richly would any labor of ours be repaid, should but one single person be thus warned against the dangers of some hour, now seemingly afar off, and be rescued through the warning!

"Putting away lying, speak every man truth with his neighbor." It is esteemed in the world the most extreme of insults, to be termed a liar. Few men of the world will endure it without open and violent resentment: it is held by many to be a sufficient justification for a sudden and brutal blow. One might imagine that the sin was so unusual and monstrous, as to inspire by its very name an universal contempt and disgust. Undoubtedly, too, the actual, direct utterance of what is known to be absolutely untrue, is not a frequent occurrence amongst persons of good reputation. But every one who is a liar, has become a liar by degrees, and once, perhaps, could furnish better proofs of his integrity, than signs of wrath or acts of violence, when it was called in question. So deep, however, is the disgrace of lying, beyond that of many other sins, a disgrace affixed to it, not because it is worse than many others, but because it is fatal to the interests of society; so wide is that concurrence in condemning it, which proceeds from the necessity of being able to trust one another; that it is one of the last sins of the same rank which any of us would be willing to acknowledge. Many transgressions, long since repented, a man would not unwillingly pour into the ear of his nearest friend; transgressions which, however forbidden by the law of God, are not severely condemned by the prevailing sentiment of worldly honor. I suppose that even a Christian who, in the days of his impenitence, might have been a party to a duel, would freely narrate the transaction afterwards, though with marks of horror and of agonizing remorse. It is very doubtful whether the same

Christian could bring himself with equal ease to relate that, at some other time, he had spoken a mean and deliberate falsehood. Such a falsehood, however, is beyond all doubt, the cause of far less guilt than a consent to shed the blood of a fellow-mortal, or our own, in unlawful and murderous combat. But so it is, that few are ready to confess themselves liars at any past period; and as this is also, of all sins, almost the most difficult of proof, because the intention to deceive must be shown, it is a sin which must generally be left to the tribunal of the individual conscience. Every one of us, old or young, knows well whether he himself is accustomed to speak the honest and entire truth, in all his intercourse with his fellow-men; not on very solemn occasions merely, nor when no inducement is offered to speak otherwise; but throughout, in secret conversation, or in trifling affairs, and when shame or interest seems to forbid that all should be told. False pretences, a more common form of the same sin, are perhaps less often hidden from the perception of those to whom they are offered, than those imagine who strive thus to cloak their selfish purposes. We see, from day to day, representations by which few are deceived, and which yet involve more or less of the guilt of intentional deception. There is, it is true, a considerable separation between the direct lie which is designed to injure, and many of these subordinate forms of misrepresentation. But the sentiment of the sacredness of truth is no more, unless the truth be always spoken, directly and indirectly, nor unless, if we wish to conceal, the modes of honest concealment be chosen. Reflect on the manner in which the habit of falsehood is acquired; and it is commonly acquired at an early period of life, if ever. Would not the very slightest encouragement be sufficient to secure its growth in childhood? If a child should chance to perceive in a parent, or a teacher, or some respected friend, the smallest departure from strict openness with a view to mislead, will he be slow to learn the lesson? If a lad, employed in a shop or a manufactory, should be directed to place upon some article a stamp importing that it was what it was not, or was made where it was not made, or to copy an advertisement, stating what he knew to be not true in the common acceptation of language, could you wonder to find him also framing his own statements, as to his own conduct, with a similar design and in a similar manner? Perhaps, if an inquiry could be diligently prosecuted, we should discover that the strength of those habits of falsehood which in the young are the foundation of all future evils, has been received from some practices which run through large portions of society, and are not felt in their real enormity. If you would preserve the holiness of truth unimpaired in the youthful mind, you must evince that you revere it, and you must require that it be revered, on all occasions alike, the more serious and the more trivial. As instances in which it seems sometimes to be too little regarded, we may mention the practices of hastily promising things which we scarcely expect to remember; entering into small pecuniary engagements with great carelessness as to the issue, if our own interests or credit be not impaired; stating facts with some perversion or exaggeration, which, in the end, sometimes leads to perjury; requiring broad and sweeping promises, whether of children or of older persons, where we can hardly hope for their full execution; and availing ourselves of the weaknesses of men to persuade them to steps which otherwise, if urged with the statement of our true motives, they might refuse. Such practices undermine all around us the sentiment of truth; and if they could be justified, it would be hard not to excuse some direct falsehoods, uttered for the sake of avoiding loss or shame. From a falsehood uttered to avoid loss or shame to a falsehood uttered to secure gain or honor, and from this to any other falsehood whatever, the way is short and simple and easy. Therefore, though every one of us might reject with disdain the charge of lying, let us all see well, as in the sight of God, that we put away lying itself with far more disdain.

"Be ye angry," the Apostle proceeds, "be ye angry, and sin not; let not the sun go down upon your wrath; neither give place to the devil." Anger is mentioned as a natural emotion, which has its own times and occasions of just exercise, but which is to be held under careful restraint, since it readily passes into sin; since it is unworthy to last beyond the first necessary glow; and since it is afterwards a mighty snare of the tempter. Justifiable anger is either so mere a flush, or else so subdued a flame, that perhaps there is little danger of confounding it with that which is deeply guilty. Almost all the anger which we notice in others, is evidently wrong; and when we perceive its hatefulness in them, let the dreadful light flash back upon ourselves. The best preservative may be, to remember this saying of St. Paul, which implies that, when we are angry, the devil is at hand, as if in an hour of advantage. He is the author of divisions amongst friends; and anger is his instrument. He rejoices in violence and bloodshed; and these must always begin with anger. The darkest deeds which the laws of God and man condemn and pursue with all their punishments, are those which are done by the angry. Of all anger, too, that is the most hateful on which the sun goes down and rises and goes down, and completes his annual course and goes down upon it still; that flame which, when years have gone by, still lives under its ashes, sparkles up at a touch, and will not even then be quenched by all the waters of charity or forgetfulness. May God preserve us from such anger, as from the guilt and the bondage of him who was a murderer from the beginning!

"Let him that stole, steal no more;" and of course we may freely add, let him that never stole forbear, for his soul's sake. Nor let him esteem the warning so utterly needless, as to refuse it his patient attention. Except the few unhappy outcasts, who from infancy are trained up in the very midst of vice, no person has laid hands on the property of another, who would not once have spurned the suggestion of stealing, with somewhat of the same scorn and abhorrence, with which you listen to such a word. But, from time to time, some act of theft is traced to some one who would never have been suspected; and then we all tremble to think how near us so wretched a guilt may walk; and we understand more of the snares by which the way of the children of man is encompassed. Then, too, we mourn that the voice of admonition could not have been heard in season. The truth probably is, that the crime of theft is exceedingly, almost incredibly, frequent. Besides the vast number of instances which crowd our prisons, how often is the guilt suppressed! How seldom is a first offence brought before the tribunals of justice! In how many families and places of business will several occurrences of this kind be painfully remembered, weakening all confidence except that which has been tried by time, and often reviving associations of peculiar sadness! One of the most appalling tests is afforded by a very common event; the accidental loss of a sum of money, or of some article of value. Of such losses, which are constantly occurring, how few are followed by restoration, even when every search is tried, and when the lost article cannot but have been found! I hope that the mention of such a thing will not be deemed trifling, when it is remembered that in each of these instances in which no effort is made to discover the loser, an actual theft is committed; and that he who will commit such a theft will probably commit another, if there be a slight temptation and no apparent possibility of discovery. Besides, all deceptions in trade, all transactions through which that comes into the possession of one man which ought to have been in the possession of another, involve the same guilt somewhere, and prove the same character. If, then, we could distinguish in our own minds between the act and the disgrace, or if the disgrace were always sure to follow the act, a melancholy view might be unfolded, and we might cease to reckon this portion of the apostolic command in the text amongst the words which have not been needed by Christian congregations since the days of the first emancipation from heathenism.

Little more, however, can be said, than to repeat the commandment of God, which every Sunday is heard in our churches, and to add the solemn sanctions which he has added to that commandment. "Thou shalt not steal." "Neither thieves, nor covetous, nor drunkards, nor revilers, nor extortioners, shall inherit the kingdom of God." Let the young hear it; and let them be early taught to feel that his eye is about their path, and that he knoweth their thoughts long before. Let them learn how dreadful and wretched a fate it is, to be covered with shame, thrust from society, and shut up in the gloom of a prison, with the infamous and the desperate. Then let them be told that, if the guilty can escape all human knowledge, they are but going on under the knowledge of the all-seeing God, to shame that will never cease, to the prisons where the souls of the lost await the day of eternal judgment, to the abodes of the devil and his angels. Fill them with horror rather than with scorn; and if there come under their eyes one of those foolish but sometimes to them too fascinating books, in which robbery is invested with a kind of wild and adventurous dignity, tear aside the veil; show them the brutal ruffian and the miserable pilferer in their true dress; show them the gaol, the scourge and the gallows; show them the deplorable life of one whom no man can trust; show them the awful death of one of whom the Most High has said that he shall not enter into His kingdom.

"Let no corrupt communication proceed out of your mouth, but that which is good to the use of edifying." Decency or purity of conversation, that we rise no higher at present, is the great agency through which our social intercourse is enlisted on the better side. We must be instruments of benefit or of harm to each other; and although the evil which is in the heart may not always rise to the lips, there is no guilt of the lips which does not proceed from guilt of the heart. Our thoughts are known to our Maker only; and many of our words are known to none but him and our nearest associates. It is sometimes remarked, that in conversing with a Christian minister, men are careful to display only their best feelings in their purest language. Oh, would they but remember that He, whose servants they thus respect, is ever at hand; and that there is not a word of their mouths, but he knoweth it altogether! The profane oath; the jest at which you blush even while you laugh; the rough and low mode of expression, which seems to defile and brutalize every subject; the unfeeling ridicule, whose only apology against the charge of utter heartlessness, is in the confession of utter thoughtlessness; these, and all other forms of corrupt communication, belong to no single class of society. It is not the rules of grammar or of rhetoric that make a refined conversation: abundant vulgarity is found amongst the rich and exalted, who are without the fear of God; and a pure and noble chasteness of speech marks the lowliest of the godly. True purity in word is the effect of purity of thought; while corrupt communication not only proceeds from corruption of heart, but creates it anew, and spreads it all around. It hardly need be added, that what is thus true of speech, must be even more true of writing. Corrupt companions and corrupt books are much more to be dreaded than flames or poisons. Shun them for yourselves. Shun them for your children. Be not, yourselves, not in the slightest measure, partakers in such iniquity; not even by one jest that borders on indecency; not even by permitting such discourse in your presence.

These remarks on some of these sins which are grossest in their form, and most frightful in their ultimate results, must not be so perverted as if to escape from such crimes were enough to form the smallest excuse for the neglect of the far higher claims made by the gospel of God upon the heart and all its affections; nor as if we had touched more than the surface of human sinfulness. These crimes are but the boldest and foulest shapes of sin—it has many a shape beside; and all must be renounced if we would enter at the strait gate which leads to glory. But since, even in these boldest and foulest shapes, it lurks often amongst us, and not seldom lifts up its head, these are not to be disregarded in the search for subtler dangers. There is no security for virtue and good morals, except in obedience to the Gospel, in submission to the Holy Spirit. He who, with an honest and humbled heart, enlists himself in the cause of Christ, and prays for the renewal of his own soul by the grace of God, is the best champion against vice, and the only one who himself is safe. As falsehood, and wicked anger, and theft, and corrupt communication fled before the Gospel, till the Apostle could say, "and such were some of you, but ye are washed, but ye are sanctified, but ye are justified, in the name of the Lord Jesus, and by the Spirit of our God;" so, still they flee from the individual Christian, and take their abode with the youthful scorner and the aged hypocrite.

SERMON IV.

CONSCIOUSNESS OF SIN.

St. Luke, xv. 21.

"I have sinned."

They are words which scarcely any human lips will refuse to utter. No mortal ever passed the gate of death at an age later than infancy, who would not have acknowledged, when he thought of appearing before an eternal Judge, that he had sinned, and broken the divine commandments. They are words which are constantly uttered, not only in prayer and solemn confession, but substantially in the intercourse of men with men, and in that of the heart with itself. "There is no man that sinneth not," says Solomon; and all ages and all tongues accept the humbling confession, which, while it embraces each individual, embraces him along with all the rest. For that very reason, it is so easy.

6

But the consequences which it brings with it are vast and important, beyond all utterance. The truth which each one thus owns for himself and for all mankind, expresses more than it has ever entered into the profoundest or most pious mind to fathom. Sin, its nature, its guilt, its results, its bondage; the possibility of deliverance; the way of deliverance, if it be possible; the justice of God; his mercy; the reconciliation between them; forgiveness; the restoration of the sinner to such a state that he shall be as if he had not sinned; all these topics come crowding upon us, when we fix our eyes upon the one awful truth that men are sinners. With the admission of that fact, every thing is changed; the past, the present, the future, must be read in its light: our own destiny is all governed by our moral state, and our moral state is stamped by the admission of our sinfulness; so that if there be still a hope, it is quite another hope than that which we could have maintained, had sin never fastened itself upon our souls.

Let us consider for a little time the simple fact, which is, as each will acknowledge, a part of the history of every one of us, so that each can truly say, and does readily say, "I have sinned;" and afterwards, let us pass on to some of its consequences. May God so write his laws upon our hearts, that we may know our sins and be prepared for his mercies!

"Sin is not imputed where there is no law." The very idea of such a thing as sin implies that there has been a rule of duty which has been transgressed. If God had given us no commands; if he had neither revealed to us his will through his inspired servants, nor inscribed it upon our conscience, we could not have been sinners. When we acknowledge that we have sinned, we own that we have known the right way, while we have followed the wrong. The brute can have no such knowledge when he obeys his passionate, animal instincts: there is for him no such restraint of moral law; since there is nothing in his nature which could respond to its injunctions. The infant has a nature which is subject to moral laws; but as yet he is incapable of knowing them: they are to him as if they had not been revealed; and therefore, he is guilty of no actual sin. But as he ripens, and his nature develops itself, the rule of right and wrong is also disclosed as it is written within; and he hears, too, the voice of God through his word, and feels its power and authority. The more his understanding expands, the more clearly does he perceive his duty; the more distinctly does he feel himself condemned when he goes astray. I speak now of nothing concerning which there can be a dispute, but only of that which, when we own that we have sinned, we necessarily acknowledge by that very confession. We do not mean that we have sinned in doing that which we did not know to be evil, or in leaving undone that which we did not know to be good. The law was before us when we transgressed; and we beheld it as the will of our Maker, and as our duty; and if there was ignorance, it was the ignorance of inattention, of neglect, of forgetfulness, of indifference, which itself was sinful.

Here, then, let us stand still for a moment. Do you wonder that, when the Lord had said to Adam and Eve, "Of the tree of the knowledge of good and evil, ye shall not eat, but of every tree of the garden beside, ye may freely eat," they yet ate of that one tree, and broke that one commandment? Do you wonder that the Israelites, after just hearing from the voice of God on Sinai, the awful words, "Thou shalt not make unto thee any graven image, nor the likeness of any thing in heaven or in earth; thou shalt not bow down to them, nor worship them," should have made a golden calf, and cried, "These be thy gods, O Israel?" Do you wonder at every open and bold defiance or denial of the word of God, and every literal violation of his direct and undoubted injunction? But such, just such, is the nature of all sins which are committed in the face of the plain testimony of conscience. Of these alone we speak at this moment. There are secret faults; secret, perhaps, even to him by whom they are cherished, while he knows not the law by which they are forbidden, or while it is banished for the time from his recollection. There is such a thing, too, as a conscience seared, as if with a hot iron; so that it feels nothing at the approach, the thought, or the commission of iniquity. But we are now concerned with those who, acknowledging that they have sinned, acknowledge that they knew the commandment which they violated. They heard, too the voice from Sinai; they heard the voice which had spoken in Eden: they were aware of the terrors of the law: they listened to the words, "thou shalt surely die:" they knew, too, the love of their God; that he had made them, and endued them with all their powers, and placed them upon this earth, as in a fair garden, and given them all things richly to enjoy, and blessed them with an immortal nature, and promised glory, honor and immortality if they would but continue in well-doing. Against all this they have offended: they have lifted their hearts and hands in rebellion against such power and goodness. Each single act of conscious sin was such a rebellion. Let every excuse be alleged; let all be said which can be truly said to lighten the horror of our disobedience; but on the other side, let all be well considered which aggravates the offence. The mercies of our past days; the love of our heavenly Father; the happiness of being at peace with him; the real excellence of all goodness; the smallness of any temptation by which we have been led astray; the dreadful ingratitude of all sins; the loathsomeness and abominable blackness of many of them, even in our own sight; all must be remembered also when we are disposed to plead our own weakness, or any palliating circumstances of our guilt.

We are obliged, when we would estimate the character of sin in itself, to fix our eyes thus upon some one single act, and to make it clear to us, as the direct refusal of a direct command. God speaks, and we will not hear. God gives a law, and we violate it with full intention. If but one such act were done, it is plain that it breaks the bond of allegiance, duty and love.

On one such decision, all might be suspended. We could not justly arraign the divine justice, if it were announced to us when one such command should be given, that obedience in that one instance should make us forever secure, and that disobedience in that one instance should be fatal. There was no injustice when such a sentence was, as it were, suspended from the branches or fastened around the trunk of the forbidden tree in Paradise. One trial might be enough. If disobedience were not the act of a moment, obedience also would be even easier. In itself, it is always easier to refrain from a guilty act, than to perform it; and so we should find it, had we no sinful inclinations. One single sin, committed with deliberation and full consciousness, is a high act of exceeding wickedness, and must separate man from God, and might work in the heart of man himself such a change from purity to ever increasing guilt, as he could never have understood but by dreadful experience.

But now multiply this one act by—what number? How shall we number what are more in number than the hairs of our heads? If it be a sin to use the Sabbath-day without regard to God and his commands and service; if it be a sin not to keep it holy from its dawn to its close, what shall be said of those who do not religiously observe one of its hours, and who have not for many years observed thus a single hour of a single Sabbath? For every idle word that men shall speak, they shall give account in the day of judgment. Who can remember his own idle words, which have gone from him like the breath of the wind that stirs the leaves, and is away? How numberless are the acts, the sayings and the thoughts for which, from day to day, the heart of a Christian condemns him as soon as they can have been recorded in the book of the divine account? What part in the life of an ungodly man is not part of one great sin; that of withholding himself and all which is within him from the service of his Creator? My friends, from the very thought of this process of reckoning up our sins, each one of them such as has been described, we all recoil with dismay. God only knows them all: he only can reckon them; but with him they are reckoned and recorded, just as they were; each as distinctly as if it had been the only one. Who art thou that darest, in thine own righteousness, to meet that complete record? If one sin could so condemn the soul, who now shall stand?

The simple, yet most awful and overwhelming fact, is that we have thus sinned; not by one act, nor by ten, nor by a hundred; but by acts, words and thoughts innumerable; not merely by any succession of these, which can be measured, but by the habitual disobedience of a heart that loved not God and cared not for his commandments. He who honestly and humbly says, "I have sinned," will, if he pursues the reflection, confess that his sins have been more than he can number, and greater than he can express.

If this be so, let us next reflect upon the consequences, the necessary consequences, of this truth; and let us be prepared to view them without disguise. Are we thus sinners? Then, there is an end, an end forever, of all hope of justifying ourselves before the God of perfect holiness. We cannot undo the past. We have not the power to blot one single record from the pages of that book, which is but the true history of all human things as they are in the divine judgment and remembrance. Whatever hope the transgressor may venture to indulge, it is not the hope of the innocent. Let this be impressed upon the heart; for upon this depends all appreciation of the Gospel. It is a remedy for sin: it is good tidings to the guilty. It has no special significance for the blameless, if such there were. They would of themselves fulfil that law of God, the fulfilling of which is love. They would need no pardon; and the Gospel reveals a pardon. They could not repent; and the Gospel calls to repentance. Were we such, we could not be those whom the Son of man came to save; for he came into the world to save sinners; and thus you see the infinite importance of distinctness in this view of your condition. You must not begin upon one foundation, and attempt to finish upon another. You must not endeavor to combine things which are opposite and utterly irreconcileable. Salvation is only for those who are in danger or are lost. None are lost, none are in danger, but those who have incurred by sin the sentence of divine justice; who, having broken the commandment, are liable to its penalties. These are in danger, these are lost, unless they shall be saved by mercy. Now, ascertain your own condition, and be satisfied whether you are to be saved as sinners, or whether you can meet your God in judgment, as righteous and holy, and needing no salvation. But you have acknowledged that you were sinners. Henceforth, therefore, look only for mercy, and never be tempted to forget for one moment, or one thought, that all must be of grace, that all good which can be allotted you is undeserved.

Another consequence will immediately follow; contentment with our lot. If we have sinned, it is a mercy that we are not visited with punishment. Had it pleased God to bring upon us tribulation and wrath, could we have justly murmured? But he has crowned our lives with his goodness, and made the history of every day a record of his bounties. He has preserved and defended us; has given us all for which we so much value our life, and has filled our memory with recollections which we would not give up, and shed over the future a light of hope which always cheers us onward. We are chastened also; we suffer; perhaps we suffer much; but we do not suffer as we justly might; and we know that all our sufferings may, through the mercy of our heavenly Father, be exchanged for joys unspeakable, and be the means of adding rapture to those joys at last. In the very thought, then, that we have sinned, is the foundation for a holy cheerfulness, a peaceful submission, and a boundless, humble gratitude. The least mercies are more than our merit: "it is of the Lord's mercies that we are not confounded." Let every breath of discontent be silent, and let us rejoice because as prisoners of hope, we are still in the land of the living, surrounded with innumerable comforts and delights, and permitted to lift up our eyes to the land of eternal glory.

If you can say, too, and must say, from your heart, "I have sinned," you must feel towards your fellow-men as a sinner towards sinners. You know very well that it is as true of all the rest as of you, although you cannot know their peculiar transgressions in the same manner as your own. Each one of all these multitudes, when he lays his hand upon his heart with devout sincerity, and when he bows before his Maker in secret, or when he hides himself, as it were, from the terrors of the wrath to come, confesses that he has sinned; and in this you and he are equals; not in the number and degree of your trespasses, but in the fact that both have broken the law, and are not innocent. But if all were alike sinners, there is an end also of all proud elevation of ourselves above our fellow-men, and all contemptuous repulses of publicans and sinners from our side; and there is an end, too, of all extravagant and unbounded admiration, or unhesitating, thorough imitation of those who, like us, have sinned against heaven and in the sight of our heavenly Father. Rather, must he who feels his own sinfulness, and hears from the hearts of his fellow-men the acknowledgment of them, hasten to find the remedy, and then to make it known, and apply it wherever those are found who are but willing to receive it at his hands. The sick man who has just recovered from his malady through the power of some blessed medicine, will speed to bear it to the bedsides of those who are dying with the same malady. He will not dream of being proud of his recovery, or of scorning their sufferings. He will but say, "Taste, and see how gracious the Lord is:" "Look up like me to the brazen serpent, and like me be healed."

But first of all, though this be the last in our present reflections, first of all, if you must say that you have sinned, seek for yourselves the remedy. This is not a confession to be made, and then suffered to echo away and die away, without result. When you say, "I have sinned," it is as if you said, "I am dying;" "I am drowning;" or, "My clothes are on fire." The very next thought, following as swiftly as the cry for relief follows the sharp pang of distress, should be, "What must I do to be saved from my sin and all its woe?" God has not left us without a remedy: there is balm in Gilead; there is a Physician there; forgiveness is within the reach of the guilty; the Son of Man is come to seek and to save. Perhaps you have found in him, not wisdom alone, through his instructions; but righteousness, in your justification from your guilt, through his precious blood; and sanctification, through the Holy Spirit, which is his gift; and redemption, in hope of the glory which shall be revealed. If it be so, seek, like your Lord, to save those who still are ready to perish. If it be not so, tarry not, I beseech you, but feel your sin as a burden too grievous to be borne; feel it as a torture and a poison, till it is taken away by the Lamb of God. I call you back, once more, to the simple statement, that you have sinned; I suppose it to be one which you cannot but utter; and I ask of every one of you who is not prepared to die, every one who has not that hope in Christ which maketh not ashamed, can you confess that you have sinned, and seek no pardon and no deliverance? If you thus remain, there is but one path before you. Sin will cling to you to the end. It will be like a cumbering load upon your conscience. It will be like a consuming venom in all your members, and in your heart. It will accompany you into eternity; and when the sins of all the penitent have been washed away, and they stand in joy before the everlasting throne, you will have only to fulfil eternally that righteous sentence, "the wages of sin is death." God grant us all repentance unto life!

SERMON V.

CHRISTIAN POVERTY.

St. Luke, xvi. 20, 21.

"And there was a certain beggar named Lazarus, which was laid at his gate, full of sores, and desiring to be fed with the crumbs which fell from the rich man's table; moreover, the dogs came and licked his sores."

It was the plain design of him who uttered the parable of the rich man and Lazarus, to place before his hearers, at the beginning, a picture of the lordliest wealth on one side and the most abject poverty on the other. To represent the poor, he chose one of the poorest of mankind. Lazarus was not simply a poor man, not simply one who needs and receives alms, but one who asks them and depends upon them, and has no other resource; a beggar. He was not only a beggar, but sick and lame, and unable to move himself; so that he was laid by others at the gate of the rich man, who fared every day so sumptuously. He was not only a beggar there, but a beggar whose wants were even there and thus but ill supplied; for he desired to be fed with the crumbs which fell from the rich man's table. He was not only infirm; but his infirmities were of that class which are most repulsive, even to the compassionate. He was not only an object of human pity, but he failed, it would seem, to obtain that pity; for the dogs came and licked his sores, while no one was near to drive them away, and to bind up the poor victim of disease.

I know not how a painter, who wished to harrow up the feelings of mankind by the representation of squalid want, could better accomplish his design, than by sketching a scene like this. It is impossible to bring it strongly before our imagination without pain and compassion, and every thing short of horror. But let us now regard what, by this representation, our Saviour must have intended to teach us concerning poverty.

He must have meant to teach us that the ills of poverty are not intolerable. By a large proportion of mankind they are more dreaded than any other evils. That deep poverty does include privation of many real and valuable blessings, and exposure to some grievous calamities, is not to be denied by any one who knows how to appreciate the bounties of our heavenly Father. It is made the very duty of all who enjoy the blessings of plenty, to extend them, as far as they can, to all who are without them; so that the divine commandments themselves, imply the superior happiness of possessing those things which the very poor lack, and which the more prosperous are required to impart. The prayer of Agur, "Give me neither poverty nor riches," is a part of the Holy Scriptures, the prayer of a wise and pious man, recorded for our study and imitation, at least in its spirit. No one could ever suppose that the lot of Lazarus was intended by our Saviour to represent one of earthly happiness. "Thou in thy lifetime," said Abraham to the rich man, "receivedst thy good things, and Lazarus evil things." There are evil things in such deep poverty: no one can wish it: all ought to strive to shun it; and parents have a special assurance that, in the ways of godliness they shall avert it from their children. "Never," says the Psalmist, "saw I the righteous forsaken, nor his seed begging their bread." He does not deny that it might have occurred; but in a long life it had not fallen under his observation; and it must be an unusual and a mysterious dispensation, if it occur at all. To such an one as Lazarus, it may be the consequence of the guilt of a parent, or of his own guilt in earlier days, long since repented. But, whether it be thus, or whether God, in his all-wise Providence, should sometimes, though seldom, visit his own servant, or the children of his servant, with extreme want, even to beggary, the blessed Redeemer here tells us that there are evils far more to be dreaded than this. For Lazarus, in the midst of all his poverty, must have had that peace which passeth all understanding. He was one of those poor, whom the Lord has pronounced blessed, because their's is the kingdom of heaven. He was no object of pity for the children of this world, could they have seen him as he was, or only of a pity which he could most largely return, while he beheld their pride and vanity. It is surely far better, even if we look only to present peace, to be with Lazarus at the gate, than with the rich man within, at his table. But few, very few, are those who are visited with poverty like that of Lazarus. The condition which is dreaded by most, is only that of dependence, or of partial privation, or of diminished comforts. This was the very state in which our Saviour himself chose to pass the time of his pilgrimage. It cannot be the chief of evils to live as He lived, or even to take our place, in some measure, with the lowly Lazarus.

Our Saviour designed to teach us that these very sufferings may be the way to heavenly glory. It was not necessary to the salvation of men that each should tread the same thorny path with Lazarus; yet by that path did Lazarus find admission to Abraham's bosom. The danger through which the rich man perished was probably in the pride of life by which he was surrounded: from *that* danger, at least, the beggar was exempt. He was, doubtless, drawn by his own wants and woes to the refuge which is open in the mercies of God for all who suffer and who pray. The Lord brings before us, in direct comparison, the lot of extreme poverty, with the glory which may follow, and the lot of wealth and luxury, with the misery to which it may conduct its sinful possessor. He does not say that such are, but only that such may be, the consequences, of one or the other earthly condition. If they may be, the wealth is far less to be valued than the dangers are to be feared; and the poverty is far less to be shunned, than the glory which may follow is to be sought. If it be but the will of God that we should suffer, we may be perfectly assured that the sufferings of the present time are capable of working out for us a far more exceeding and eternal weight of glory; and this is the truth which the poverty of Lazarus was designed to impress on all who suffer. What are the toils or distresses of the way, when the end is but safely won? From the bosom of Abraham, from the general assembly and church of the first-born, how easy will it be to look back upon the poorest lot with unutterable thankfulness that it saved us from temptations under which we might have perished! How blessed, too, must be the passage from a place in the dust to a mansion in the skies; from hunger and thirst, and cold and nakedness, to all peace and joy and triumph; from lying with brute beasts at the door of an earthly palace, to sitting down with Abraham, Isaac and Jacob, in the heavenly abodes!

But our Lord designed also to teach us all to respect the poor. He has told us that in the day of judgment he will recompense that which has been done to them, as if it had been done to himself. He, also, though he was rich, yet for our sake became poor, and dwelt amongst the children of men as one who had not where to lay his head. He gave us also in this parable the picture of one of those saints who rest with Abraham above, as, while here below, a despised beggar. It may be that any beggar whom we may pass by on the other side, is a Lazarus in spirit; one whose soul, should he sink under his sufferings, would be welcomed to the society of angels. Need it be said, then, that we must take heed that we despise not one of them? Much more than this: learn to honor, and to regard with unfeigned respect, the man who in his deep lowliness of condition, is patient, devout and poor in spirit. Christ dwells with him: he is a member of Christ: he is an heir of treasures in heaven and of a kingdom that shall not be moved. Speak not of him, think not of him, as one whom it is painful to behold, because he is in any thing like Lazarus; but accustom yourselves to look through all this outward want or deformity or weakness or disease, to the inner man of the heart, which in the sight of God is of great price. There are last that shall be first. They are the children of one Father, whom it is your highest privilege to call your Father who is in heaven. Lighten their sorrows, and when you can, remove their burdens. And since you cannot be sure who amongst the poor are, and who are not, like

Lazarus in heart, suppose in charity that those of whom you know no ill, may be like him, and take heed that you despise them not.

Our Lord unquestionably, also, would teach the necessity of almsgiving; of that charity which actually relieves the poor. It is not positively said that Lazarus suffered through the hardness of the heart of that rich man at whose gate he lay; but such is certainly the general impression received from the picture. It could not have been that the pious beggar should be left there to desire the crumbs from the table, and to welcome the kindness of brute animals, unless he had been forgotten or despised by the lordly host and guests within. In this view, what a miserable thing is wealth with avarice, or wealth with luxury and softness of living and hardness of soul! After a little while, all is changed: and the beggar sits down with Abraham at the heavenly banquet, while the rich man implores in vain one drop of water, to cool his tongue and allay his torment. Had he but thought, in the day of his visitation; had he but felt for his suffering, perishing fellow-man, his heart might have become softened to the calls of God, and he might have passed from one duty to another, till he also was prepared for the world of everlasting love.

But, "he who loveth not his brother whom he hath seen, how can he love God whom he hath not seen?" Remember the poor, if you would be graciously remembered, now and in the account. "Blessed are the merciful, for they shall obtain mercy." We know very well that extreme poverty is, to a large extent, the fruit of vice or of sloth, or of great incapacity for the common transactions of life. A prejudice against the poor is thus nourished where there is, as in human nature there always is, too ready a disposition to withhold. We almost take it for granted that those who seem to need assistance are but imposing upon our humanity. Certainly, all are not to be supplied. It is a duty to examine, if we can, and be satisfied. It is, it seems to me, not only not a duty to assist, but a duty not to assist the vicious in their vices, and we confer no benefit when we uphold the slothful in their slothfulness. The principle has the authority of the apostle: "If any man will not work, neither should he eat," from the charitable contributions of his brethren. But is the great duty of relieving the poor at an end; that duty which runs all through the Scriptures; which is required in so many forms of exhortation and of praise, and which has such blessed promises of final acceptance and reward? Are there none for whom it can be performed? Have the words lost their force, "the poor ye have always with you, and when ye will, ye may do them good?"[1] Oh, no: there are poor enough, whom we have no right to charge with misconduct, or against whom it is now too late to make the charge, since the mischief can no longer be undone. Even if all who suffer like Lazarus had been entirely unlike him, in character, yet amongst those whose sufferings are less aggravated, amongst those who bear much, but are not forsaken, are found a very considerable proportion of the excellent of the earth. True charity reaches far beyond the mere supply of food and raiment. It desires to afford every consolation, every convenience, every advantage which we ourselves enjoy. If the *poorest* should cease amongst us, the *poor* would still remain; for in that sense, which concerns our duty, all are poor, to whom we can render aid, service or comfort. But without looking farther than to those who, indeed, like Lazarus, have in their lifetime received their evil things, let us not restrain the hand of pity, except where we absolutely must. The beggar whom you do not know to be otherwise, may be a Lazarus; and it is better that our charity should go astray, being charity still, than that our judgment should be right, and our hearts become deafened and deadened.

Our Lord would teach us how strangely different is the light in which our condition may now and here appear from that in which it is seen by those who dwell where all is light. An illustration may often be found in what we see within our own earthly experience. Two children of different families, for instance, may grow up in the same neighborhood. One is left an early orphan, dependent entirely on distant friends or strangers, and exposed to all those struggles which, when we look on a little one of our own, would, even if only imagined, melt us to tears. The other has all the care of parents, who live only for him, who lay up treasures for him, and who study nothing so much as to secure to him the largest possible measure of human happiness. Years pass by; and we look back upon this difference, and can now trace the results. The poor and friendless orphan has reached the end of all his difficulties; has ripened amidst the storms of adversity, into a vigorous, successful and virtuous man; and sees in the very disadvantages, as they seemed, of his early lot, his defence against many fatal temptations. That discipline made him strong, and now makes him happy. The indulged and prosperous child of wealthy parents, always accustomed to the gratification of his desires, lived to lament that he had not rather suffered in his youth; to lose, through habits of reckless folly, all which he had enjoyed; and to be pointed out in society, as one whom his own good fortune, as it is termed, had ruined. This is no very unfrequent spectacle, and it tells us how rashly we judge, when we presume that calamity for a while will be misfortune at last. So may angels observe the lot of mortals. We all are children: we see only the passing day, but not its consequences. *They* know that this whole life of ours has all its importance from its connection with the life, the everlasting life, which is to follow. To be trained up here under the severe discipline of want, sickness or scorn, may be the surest and the fittest method through which the soul can be preserved from far more dreadful evils, and prepared for a celestial inheritance. It is hard to our view to be deprived of so much which makes this life pleasant; of health, of friends, of respect, of knowledge, even of comfortable food and raiment; for none of these blessings were the lot of Lazarus. If this life were all, such an one would be indeed, of all men, most miserable. That we should despise these earthly blessings, is certainly not required; but only that we should submit, when they are withheld by our heavenly Father, and hold fast our confidence in his goodness. Though we should go to our graves without them, it is but the lot which he has appointed for myriads. He appointed it for one, and doubtless for many others, whom angels welcomed at the hour of departure, and conducted to the mansions of perpetual peace. Thus can he educate for heaven.

And now, as the appropriate close and result of all these reflections, choose you this day whom you will serve, and whether you will live for this world or for the eternal kingdom of your Lord and Saviour. Which is now the most happy, which has been for many centuries; Lazarus, or the rich man at whose gate he lay? They are separated by a gulf which cannot be crossed; and Lazarus, who had his evil things here, is comforted, and he who had his good things here, is tormented. Your choice does not lie between the earthly lot of the rich man and that of Lazarus; but if it did, could your reason hesitate in its decision? Better, far better, it must say, to suffer any thing here which can be followed by eternal glory, than to enjoy any thing here which can but end in the misery of those who are forever lost. Be content, then, with your lot, whatever it be; and ask no more of earthly ease or riches or honors, than just so much as the Lord knows to be best; just so much as may be united with safety from the temptations of the world and sin; just so much as may work together to make you meet for an inheritance with saints in light. Go not with those who will be rich, and fall into a snare; shut not up your hearts against the poor: keep a good conscience, cost whatever it may: refuse the invitation of vain and dissipating pleasures: love to refresh the hearts and soothe the sorrows of the saints of God: hold the day of death and the day of judgment always in view: and pray, for yourselves and for your children, that you may be willing rather to suffer the loss of all things, than to be numbered with those who have their portion in this life alone.

SERMON VI.

DISCIPLINE OF AFFLICTION.

Psalm cxix. 67.

"BEFORE I WAS AFFLICTED, I WENT ASTRAY; BUT NOW HAVE I KEPT THY WORD."

THE benefits of affliction have always been the subject of religious observation. They are most frequently and most feelingly mentioned by those who have themselves known, in their deep experience, what it was to walk humbly with their God along the valley of weeping; or by those who have watched with a spiritual eye the effect of the visitations of God on such as he has loved and chastened. The young, perhaps, can hardly understand it; and the thoughtless and the worldly will not. But the time comes when each of us must place at his own lips the cup which has passed from one to another of his fellow-men. Then, many, many learn, even for the first time, how God can be gracious, most gracious of all, in the midst of his most distressing allotments. Then, with a peace such as the world never gave, they all lift up, though in tears, the song of the Psalmist: "Before I was afflicted, I went astray; but now have I kept thy word."

Generation after generation, such is the experience of mankind. But when such a truth is so often presented to our view in the Holy Scriptures, it is not merely that it may be confirmed by experience. It is rather, that the experience already won by so many might be made needless for many others. It is that we might not go astray before we are afflicted. It is that, being taught by the lessons which those have learned, who, after being afflicted, have kept the word of God, we might not only know the place of refuge for our souls in the time of trouble, and the benefit of divine chastisement, but also might anticipate that time, and find peace, even in our prosperity. Why should we go astray till affliction comes with its sorrowful instruction? Why should we not keep the word of truth and righteousness, and have all its comfort in the day of evil, unmixed with the pain of remorseful recollections?

But if it be too late for this, and we have gone astray, and are afflicted already, then the example of the Psalmist may yet guide us to a peace, more humbling but still divine. No where, indeed, is the divine might of the religion of the Gospel more manifest or more glorious than when it binds up the broken-hearted, and comforts those who mourn, whatever be the peculiar character of their sorrow. How wonderful, yet how certain, the power which changes the darkest hours of life into the brightest, and, if we may borrow the comparison of one of the poets, reveals to us by night such heavenly worlds as were never seen during the blaze and sunshine of the day!

Let us contemplate first, the period before affliction, and then the period after; first, the period when so many go astray, and then the period when so many, through the instructive lessons of a sad experience, have learned to keep the word which alone can give us peace.

"Before I was afflicted," says the Psalmist, and with him thousands on thousands: "before I was afflicted I went astray." There is, for most men, a certain portion of their lives which might be described as the time before they were afflicted. Some, indeed, know sorrow almost from the beginning. We see early orphans. We see children who are left as the last of their family. But such bereavement is not the common lot; and even where it falls, youth, hope and a joyous temper seem to surmount all; the future still lies fair before the dreaming fancy: the mind rallies from its depression; and even those who have then been most afflicted, know not affliction as it comes at a later and riper season. Some feel, too, much more deeply than others, and it is as much the manner in which calamity affects the heart, as the calamity itself, that separates these different periods of life so broadly. Whatever be the exact character of the distinction, most of us who have lived long and known sorrow, can recall the first event which placed such a barrier between the unafflicted and the afflicted region of our history. Before we reached that point, we had enough of worldly prosperity in prospect, to be a foundation for those hopes without which the human mind has never much enjoyment. We looked forward; we had health; we had friends; our family circle was as yet unbroken; we saw no cause which should necessarily prevent the gratification of our warmest wishes; all was uncertain, but happiness far beyond our expectation, as well as sorrow which we had not conceived, might be hidden under this uncertainty, and hope suggested always all which was most flattering. Do we not constantly witness in the young a state of mind like this? Do they not hear of trouble as if it were something in which they had no concern, or which lay very far off in the future, almost beyond their sight? Does not the same disposition accompany many far onward in life, till they seem never to expect reverses and adversities? Does it not even so blind and harden some, that when adversities befall them, they still are not afflicted in soul, but pass on with just as much worldly ambition or pleasure as before? Such is the period, longer or shorter, in which the iron has not entered into the soul, and man has not been afflicted.

How beautiful, how happy, how precious in all recollection, how precious in the sight of God, would be the earlier and unafflicted portion of life, were it sanctified by the word of God and prayer; were it received and enjoyed with thanksgiving! How blessed, if, instead of going astray, the youthful heart might choose from the first, and steadfastly pursue, the straight and narrow, yet pleasant and peaceful way, of the divine commandments! How lovely and excellent is true wisdom, and how large are her promises to those who seek her early! "Length of days is in her right hand: in her left hand are riches and honor." A soul consecrated to God from youth upward; consecrated to him long before "the days in which we shall say, we have no pleasure in them;" consecrated to him while all health and vigor, and all the powers and the means of doing good are still undiminished; when there is something which we can still call our own, and some other motive than the urgent dread of a speedy summons to judgment; such a soul lays up for itself a treasure of happy remembrances, the value of which can only be fully known when they that have done good shall receive everlasting life; and they that have patiently continued in well-doing, shall have the glory, honor and immortality which they sought. Then, though the laborers who were last in the vineyard shall not lack their reward, and though all shall own that every recompense is of grace, and though there can be no pride, no envy, no scorn amongst holy and blessed spirits, yet may such as gave their youth and their prosperity to God, remember with unutterable thankfulness, how, before they were afflicted, they ceased to go astray.

Is it not better, my young friends, than to wait for the afflictions which may drive you to such a shelter? These afflictions will arrive; and their certainty is within your knowledge.

What has happened to all other mortals will happen also to you. You have no friend too dear to be one day separated from you by the grave: one must be taken, while the other remains. However robust your health may seem, it will, sooner or later, fail; and you are no more exempt than others from the more appalling forms of disease and dissolution. Look around, and see the losses and misfortunes by which so many are constantly visited; and ask yourselves whether you have any right to think that you are always to remain firm, and to enjoy your lot, and feel none of those sorrows. Your reason repels all such vain dreams of security. Will you wait, then, till the evil hour shall arrive, and then flee to the only refuge; or will you seek it now, while the goodness of God, by all its blessings, invites you to choose the better part, that shall not be taken from you?

But, alas, the too common choice is otherwise. We will not pause from our mirth and our business. We will not look into ourselves. The world draws us on, fills up our time, fixes our affections, finds us employment, affords us pleasure enough to prevent the pressing sense of the need of something higher; and thus we follow the devices and desires of our own hearts, and go astray. It is the story, more or less, of almost every human life: some wander farther and longer than others; but all wander. Even when the path, once lost, has been recovered, and we have learned to walk in the light, as children of the light, still, through the influence of the world and of that law in our members which warreth against the law of our mind, the hands hang down, the knees become feeble, and we are too readily allured away by some appearance of present repose or pleasure. Therefore, the confession is never untrue, when any one of us takes it upon his lips, be he who he may: "We have erred and strayed from thy ways like lost sheep."

Affliction is, then, the frequent instrument through which the wanderer may be restored. The process, my brethren, is plain and natural. He has been deceived: the deception must be removed. He has looked for happiness to that which cannot give him happiness. He has lived amidst his worldly enjoyments, whatever they were, as if they were to endure forever. That he may cease to trust them, they must be interrupted, or they must cease. How do you prevent the injury which a child may cause himself by sporting with dangerous weapons, except by taking the weapons from his hands?

Now, if our heavenly Father knows that we shall destroy our souls through the pride and thoughtlessness of our prosperity, how shall he save us, except by depriving us of our prosperity, wholly or partially, for a time or forever? It is the greatest of kindnesses to awaken the sleeper who lies in the way of immediate destruction; and the kindness is not the less, though his dreams should be most delightful. So God arouses us from slumbers in which we must die; and if we start up from pleasant dreams, and look on fearful realities, it is that we may escape, and be perpetually secure.

Such is, in great part, the purpose of our afflictions. They have, also, the effect, unless their operation is resisted, to soften and humble the heart, and prepare it for the reception of the will of a chastening Father. Not without cause is the trouble which he sends, compared with chastisement. The human soul, left to itself and its own propensities, is proud, self-willed and perverse. We choose to live to ourselves. We like not to acknowledge a higher law, not even the law of our Maker. The same temper appears in the uncontrolled child and in the hardened man. It is sad for the parent that he must inflict pain, or at least, must impose self-denial and restraint, before this spirit in the child can be subdued; but no kind parent will refrain from the strictness of control, or if need be, of chastisement, which cannot for the present but be grievous. So the Lord has taught us, in his holy word, that he has no pleasure in our sorrows; that he does not willingly afflict or grieve the children of men; but his very loving-kindness and tender mercy forbids that he should withhold the stroke of trouble. It falls; and human pride owns its own weakness. The heart becomes submissive, gentle, ready to hear; and on such a soil the dews of grace descend; and it yields the peaceable fruits of righteousness.

Thus to awaken and to soften, God has appointed our afflictions; and that they may be the more effectual, he has appointed that the order of their occurrence should be to us no secret. They come not to all alike. They admit of no calculation. They are here when they have been least foreseen. Sometimes they arrive after a long season of repose. Sometimes they follow one another in rapid succession, like billow after billow. No man is safe for a single day against any one of many dreadful accidents, each of which would be sufficient to overthrow all his schemes, derange his hopes, cover his domestic scene with vast distress, or remove him into eternity. Death comes like a thief in the night: health is the most uncertain of all possessions. The young and the aged sink down alternately; and none can discern who may be the next in the long procession. If such is the order of our greatest afflictions, it extends also to the less; for all earthly prospects partake of this character of anxious instability. It is the ordinance of God, fixed in his infinite wisdom; with the design that never, never should man permit himself to rest in the enjoyment of his lot, and say to himself, "thou hast much goods laid up for many years; take thine ease, eat, drink and be merry."

Since such is the appointment of Providence; since such is the necessity of affliction, to arouse and to melt; since such are its blessed effects, in leading back those who have gone astray; we shall learn to view it as indeed the highest kind of mercy. Many of you, I doubt not, already feel all this, and can look back upon the most painful periods of your lives, as those which you could least wish to be blotted from your history. Many others, as yet inexperienced in suffering, will live to learn this lesson. No chastening for the present can be joyous. No trouble can be desired. The time when it is needful, the manner in which it shall be awarded, are reserved to the judgment of God. We must leave it there; assured that our sorrows will come; and praying that we may be found to be strengthened for their arrival, with a strength which is not our own. But when they have arrived, and perhaps have passed by, not without leaving their deep and perpetual traces behind them; we can lift up our sad eyes in thankfulness, and bless our chastening Father, and confide in his goodness for the time to come. For we can perceive that it has been good for us that we have been afflicted; since before, we went astray; but now have we kept his word. If this be so certain in this world, how much more in the world where all things that have been secret shall be revealed, and we shall know as we are known! Then, we cannot doubt, the severest trials of this mortal life shall be seen to have been the tenderest proof of a boundless love; just as we know, even now, that the kindest discipline of our childhood, was sometimes that, which then it was hardest to endure!

But it is not affliction itself that can save, but only that grace of God which touches the heart through the experience of affliction. It is very possible to suffer without benefit; and he who suffers without benefit probably suffers to his own grievous loss and injury. If we are not aroused, we slumber thenceforth but so much the deeper. If we are not melted, we must be hardened. Whatever afflictions befall you, then, pray that they may work that godly sorrow which worketh repentance unto life. Ask that you may not be suffered to be like the hard, barren ground, which returns no fruit after the most careful tillage; or like the vine which, purged and pruned, yet remains only fitted to be cast into the fire. Think that he who has remained unmoved by all the blessings of prosperity, may yet keep the word of God, after he has been afflicted, but that for him who has been afflicted again and again, and in vain, all discipline is exhausted, and death alone is left.

SERMON VII.

MANLINESS IN RELIGION.

1 Corinthians, xvi. 13.

"QUIT YOU LIKE MEN, BE STRONG."

GOD gave to man, when He formed him in His own image, a certain dignity, which all his sin has not quite destroyed. He was made a little lower than the angels, and clothed with dominion over all things upon earth. Bodily strength was given him, and the countenance which looks up towards heaven, and the spirit and bearing of authority. With these corresponded certain qualities of mind; which, also, as being more boldly developed in the stronger than in the gentler sex, are commonly termed *manly*. What opportunities would have been afforded for the exercise of some of these, had man remained in innocence, it is not necessary to conjecture. But the fall has brought in death, and with it danger, temptation, trial, calamity, perplexity, suffering; and with these, the occasions for courage, firmness, endurance, energy, enterprise, steadiness, integrity; qualities, whose presence, as manly, it is not in human nature not to admire, and whose absence we must deplore, if we do not despise.

To these qualities the word of God, sanctifying the whole of our nature, makes often its appeal. "Be strong," is the exhortation of Moses to Joshua and to Israel. "Be strong, and show thyself a man," is the counsel of the dying David to Solomon. In the text, the admonition with which St. Paul closes an epistle, copious in doctrine and in directions to a church under manifold temptations, is, "watch ye, stand fast in the faith;" and then, "quit you like men, be strong." And if there be any call which ought to be often in the ears of those who, at this day, believe the word of God, such a call is this.

The Almighty God has summoned you to his own service, by a revelation from above; by the revelation of Himself through our Lord and Saviour. Like men, receive it, or reject it: receive it or reject it entirely. Be strong in unbelief, or be strong in faith; but not wavering, as the waves of the sea are driven with the wind and tossed; as the weak and unworthy halt between two opinions. Here is the first occasion for the exercise of manliness towards religion; and how many are there who, manly perhaps in many things beside, are here most irresolute, timid, hesitating, or double-minded! For one who dares boldly to deny the truth of the revelation, there are, perhaps, a hundred who only half believe, or who, while they believe, take not a single serious step in obedience to its authority. Dare you not disbelieve? Dare you not deny? Dare you not blaspheme? Does not the strength and uprightness of a man require or permit this? Then it does require submission to the word which is acknowledged to be from God; submission complete, obedient and active. Can there be any third part which is consistent with real manliness? The Christian religion is either the truth of God, given for our salvation, or it is an utter delusion or imposture. Were Christianity false, it would be manly to be a consistent infidel. If Christianity be true, it is manly to be a consistent believer. But whether it were true or false, it could not be manly to own it to be true, and at the same time to treat it as if it were a falsehood. It could not be manly to deny its truth, and yet pay it a devout reverence. Here is the greatest of all questions, to be decided for each one of us; to be decided for each one by himself: with him is the responsibility. The only path of manliness is that of prompt decision and resolute action.

Before we proceed further, let me still urge this alternative for a moment. Would I shake the adherence of any man to the Gospel, however precarious and fluctuating that adherence may be? Would I send the weakest, the most doubting, away to hopeless unbelief? Would I, by driving any to an immediate determination, loosen the little hold which religion may still have on their convictions? I apprehend no such result from that decision which I would persuade. Not a man, probably, would choose the way of death, in the spirit which I have endeavored to impress. It is because religion is not afraid of inquiry, and challenges decision, that unbelief springs up mostly on the soil of inattention. Listen to the solemn, the tremendous word, that tells you of an eternity to come, of a judgment-seat at which each shall stand, and of salvation through a Mediator between God and men, God manifest in the flesh, the man Christ Jesus. Listen, as those who know how awful a thing it is even to listen to such tidings. The obligation to listen is drawn from your own everlasting interests, and from the majesty of God. Should this be indeed a message from Him, it cannot be repulsed without the most fearful guilt. Should eternal life and death be at hazard, we could not fail to listen seriously without condemning ourselves and being condemned by our Maker. In saying this, we suppose that sufficient evidence is given to arrest attention; for we are not bound to afford even a hearing to every person or book that may come to us with a pretence of revelation. There must be something which at first constrains us to pause, and demands respect. This is demanded by the fact, that our religion has descended from our fathers; and brings with it the testimony of ages. Were it even, like other religions, a delusion, it ought not, having this testimony, to be rejected without solemn investigation. But it fixes our attention by a far stronger hold, from the very first. It is a pure, a holy religion: we see its character at a glance, and our conscience bears witness that thus must God have spoken, if he has indeed spoken to men. Thus, we are compelled to listen, and to listen with reverence; and there is none amongst us who will feel himself justified in paying less regard than this to the Gospel, even though he should be still a doubter or an unbeliever. But should he really give the solemn attention which he feels to be his duty, he would not long doubt or disbelieve. We need not fear to call upon all to decide: religion has nothing to fear from their decision. Let such be strong, and no longer halt between belief and infidelity.

Should the decision be adverse, let us imagine the consequences with one who designs to quit himself like a man. He would at once renounce all connection with the Christian religion. He would take care that none should suppose him a friend or advocate of such a system of falsehood. He would refuse to exhibit the slightest respect for its claims, or to draw the smallest encouragement from its hopes, or to yield to the least alarm at its denunciations. He would know nothing of the God of the Scriptures, but would derive all his views of his Creator and of any life to come, wholly from his own thoughts and from the contemplation of nature. Nay, he would take up arms against so mighty an error as he would deem the Christian religion; an error which had not only awakened so many vain anticipations of future bliss, but also so many fears, as vain but far more unhappy. He would have the enjoyment, whatever it might be, of fighting against all these, and perhaps of driving them from the minds of his fellow-creatures. He would show, in short, the same regard to the Gospel which is now shown by wise men to the false, foolish and often corrupting and often terrifying superstitions of the heathen. The name of blasphemer would have for him no horrors, and he would need no strong inducement to renounce, at any time, all possible part and interest in the religion of Jesus. He who should thus act would be strong in unbelief, and show himself a man by his courage and honesty in rejecting and opposing what he really deemed imposture.

You shudder, perhaps, at the imagination of such resistance to religion. But why should he pause at less than this, who has decided that religion ought to be rejected? And how shall any be excused from deciding whether it shall be rejected or received? There are, we still affirm, but two paths in which we can show ourselves men and strong. One is, decided rejection; the other, decided acceptance. You have seen what decided rejection is: now consider what it is, decidedly to receive the Gospel.

It is to show yourselves strong in the faith itself. There is no call to embrace the truth with only a half consent, as if it were but partly proved, and the mind were to be held still in a balanced state, though much inclined to belief. This may be the condition of too many minds, but it is not because such belief is sufficient, nor because the truths of the Gospel are not sufficiently clear in themselves, or not sufficiently sustained by evidence or authority. The authority on which they rest is worthy of all confidence or of none. It is no doubtful question whether the Lord Jesus was sent by the Father to be the Saviour of the world, nor what is the substance of his doctrines and commandments. Whatever he has taught, it is for us, with a single, simple heart, to follow; and what he has taught, we are not ignorant. Take the truth as he has left it, the heavenly wisdom; and bind it to your bosom. Grasp it firmly, as your life, and hold it as Peter held the hand which was stretched forth to bear him above the deep. Be not "carried about with every wind of doctrine, with sleight of men and cunning craftiness." "Contend earnestly for the faith once delivered to the saints." If we truly believe that we possess the treasure of a true revelation from God, then it is manly to maintain and defend it, for its own inestimable value, for the honor of him from whom it has come, for the gain of our own souls, and for its power to save our brethren of mankind. For such a treasure it is the noblest business of our lives to show ourselves men, and be strong.

To receive the Gospel decidedly and in a manly spirit is, next, to shrink from no duty and no sacrifice which it may require. Has the Lord spoken; the Author of my life, the Giver of my blessings, the Saviour of my soul? Then it only remains to arise and obey. The world, the flesh and the devil will all oppose it; and will present a hundred obstacles and excuses. It is not the way of the world to render *such* obedience, but only a kind of respectful treatment of the word of God; nothing bold, nothing decided, nothing cordial; and the love and the fear of the world will prompt us to do no more. A still stronger persuasion of the flesh speaks from within: it is sloth, it is selfishness: it bids us do so much, and only so much, as will satisfy the urgency of conscience, and suffice to secure us at last. The evil spirit, the great tempter, will suggest all discontented, rebellious and blasphemous thoughts; as if our Lord were a hard Master, reaping where he had not sown, and will perpetually invite us to withhold all cheerful service. Thus beset on all sides, we readily yield, the majority readily yield; and while they perhaps honor God with their lips, they follow his Gospel only so far as they dare not do otherwise. This is not to show ourselves men, with a sense of the obligations, the privileges and the just feelings of one who was made in the image of his Maker. This is not to be strong, but weaker than the reed that trembles in the wind, and can sustain nothing and produce nothing. Do not attempt the service of God in a spirit in which you would be ashamed to fulfil any other responsibility. Carry with you, as Christians, the same resolute and open manliness which all must every where honor, and which, not a few, in their earthly affairs, do indeed cultivate. In the early times of the church, many came forward with eagerness to suffer the pains and obtain the crown of martrydom. They saw that some must fall for the cause of their religion and of God; and they said, "Why should not we, if thus our brethren may be preserved? They were sometimes too eager for this exposure; but it was the same spirit which we so much admire in every soldier or citizen who steadily and bravely takes his place at the post of danger, when his country demands his service. It is the same spirit in which every one of us, who has the heart of a man, would act in defence of his own family. Let us carry the same spirit into all religious duty, and abandon forever the miserable disposition to seek or to accept excuses from that which ought ever to be welcomed as our highest privilege and blessing, the service of God just where, and in whatever manner, and to whatever extent, he has appointed.

To be strong and show ourselves men, is next, to be diligent and energetic, to be persevering and bold, to be vigorous till we are triumphant in the work which once, in the fear of God, we have undertaken. It is manly to begin well; but it is most unmanly to forsake, or negligently execute, a great task once begun. But how many have thus, and perhaps again and again, attempted and forsaken the work of salvation! I do not speak merely of those who have openly taken upon them the Christian covenant in the presence of their fellowmen, and drawn nigh to the altar. Many a man who has never declared himself, by such an act, to be pledged to the name and service of Christ, has yet, in secret, resolved to set out upon the way to eternal glory. No human eye may have discovered the resolve; but it was before the Searcher of hearts, and it was recorded in the book which shall be opened in the judgment. The way was entered in secret, but it was soon forsaken; for "the cares of this world, and the deceitfulness of riches, and the lusts of other things entering in, choked the word, and it became unfruitful." There is, no doubt, a very peculiar and a very mighty class of inducements to inconsistency and instability in religion, such as are not brought to operate upon the mind in any other sphere of action. They are simply the whole mass of the corrupt and worldly inclinations of our nature, nourished and strengthened by perpetual contact with a world that lieth in wickedness. Whatever would have persuaded us not to turn to God, will, of course, on every occasion, invite us to return to our idols. Be strong *then*, and show yourselves men, ye who have in your hearts, or in the sight of men and angels, taken up the cross of your Saviour. Remember that nothing can be changed in the value of the soul, in the love of God, in the glory of redemption, or in the solemnity of eternity. However your feelings may come and go, all these are ever the same; and when you shall be beyond all power of this present, changing scene, you will bless God forever, if you have been enabled to lay hold upon the true wisdom, and have not suffered it to depart. Persevere, and lose not the prize; for when shall man show himself a man, in strength and purpose, if not when his own soul and the souls of his brethren are at hazard, and must be saved or lost? Oh, what success, what honor, what everlasting gain, conspire to bid us be strong, and quit ourselves like men! What means of usefulness, not for this world alone, but for eternity, lie all around us! What a blessed and glorious career is before him, who labors to do all for the service of God, and for the happiness of his fellow-men, all for which he has been endowed with talents and favored with opportunities! Here, as every where, success and satisfaction are the recompense, not of half deeds, but of manly, hearty energy, industry and perseverance.

Would to God that these thoughts and words might move all of us, to submit our hearts to God, with manly humility, as we know and feel that we ought, and to seek and find, through the cross of Jesus Christ, that peace which we shall find no where but there! Would to God that those who love their Lord might be stirred up to feel their privileges and to labor as heirs of heaven! It is the word of God that gives us the command, and by giving it, promises us the strength for its fulfilment.

When He bids us be strong, it is as when Christ bade the man with the withered hand stretch forth his hand, withered as it was; and power was at once given him to obey. He calls us now to be strong, and show ourselves men, and places before us that prize of our high calling, which should be more than sufficient to awaken every nerve to its utmost energy and endurance. Heaven is the prize, heaven for ourselves, heaven for our fellow-men, heaven for those whom we lead or love. Every effort shall have its reward beyond the whole sphere of time and sorrow. We are surrounded by a cloud of witnesses who have finished their course, and reached the crown of life. They invite us onward to the same joy in which they rest from all their labors, and their works do follow them. Put off, then, the deeds of darkness, and put on the armour of light: for the night is far spent, and the day is at hand. Only a short time is left you to do the work of God: work while there yet is time. "The fearful and the unbelieving," says his word, "shall have their part with the abominable, and with murderers and liars, in the second death!" Then be not fearful nor unbelieving: fear not the little troubles that may beset the way, but be strong, "strong in the Lord and in the power of his might." The end, which is so near, will repay you for all which you can deem sacrifices. Arise, for the work is great, the time is short, the hazard is unspeakable, and the prize is eternal.

SERMON VIII.

WORLDLINESS.

St. Luke, xvii. 28, 29.

"LIKEWISE, ALSO, AS IT WAS IN THE DAYS OF LOT, THEY DID EAT, THEY DRANK, THEY BOUGHT, THEY SOLD, THEY PLANTED, THEY BUILDED; BUT THE SAME DAY THAT LOT WENT OUT OF SODOM, IT RAINED FIRE AND BRIMSTONE FROM HEAVEN, AND DESTROYED THEM ALL."

THE land of Sodom and Gomorrah was a fair and a well-watered country, along the valley of the Jordan. It had fruitful fields, populous towns, and a noble river gliding through them all, to bury itself, as it seems at first to have done, in the sands of the desert. The reaper toiled on the plain; the vine-dresser gathered the clusters on the sunny slopes of the hills; the caravan wound its way from the East; and in the streets was heard the stir of the trader and the artizan. All the pursuits and pleasures of human life were going on in those cities and their neighborhood, just as every where else amongst the haunts of men, on the day when those heavenly persons came to the tent of Abraham, and after two had departed, one remained, and announced to the patriarch the near destruction of those cities of the plain. Ardently and with holy perseverance did Abraham intercede; and his intercession would have prevailed, had not that smiling and busy scene in the plain of Jordan covered the most unparalleled horrors. The poison was too deep and thorough, and potent, to be counteracted; and the whole body must perish. There were not ten righteous persons in Sodom: if there had been ten, the city would have been rescued. There was probably none, save the family of Lot, since they alone were brought out from the impending ruin. When, in the dusk of the evening, two heavenly messengers, the same, no doubt, who had parted from Abraham, came to Lot in the gate of Sodom, the noise of business was dying away as on any other evening; the noise of merriment was rising as on any other evening; all hearts beat just as at all other times; none dreamed of danger; but with the dawn of morning came the fiery shower; and the sun rose only upon ruins smoking like a furnace, and upon the heavy and salt waters of the Dead Sea. Down to that very night, "they did eat, they drank, they bought, they sold, they planted, they builded:" their hearts were in the world, and the world went on.

When Noah had almost finished the ark, there was no sign, in heaven or earth, sufficient to convince the unbelieving that a deluge was really approaching. Day followed day, and night succeeded to night, as they had done from the creation. All predictions of divine wrath remained, till that very time, unfulfilled; and the patriarch, so far, seemed to scoffers to have spent his strength in vain and superstitious labor. They, too, ate, they drank, they married, they were given in marriage, till the flood came, and swept them all away. There was no warning but the word of God, which was proclaimed by Noah; and that warning they refused and despised. Business and pleasure, as well as folly and crime, were uninterrupted; and the face of the earth was as smiling beneath the sunbeams, as if all had been the abode of innocence and of safety.

Thus, says our Lord, thus shall it also be at the end of the world, at the coming of the Son of Man to judgment. "When they shall say, Peace and safety, then sudden destruction shall come upon them, as travail upon a woman with child; and they shall not escape." The course of the world will be what it always has been; and scoffers will ask, even to the end, "Where is the promise of his coming?" Signs indeed there may be, in the sun and moon and stars; famines and pestilences; wars and rumors of wars: these always have been, through the course of ages; and the faithful have heard and watched for his coming; but the unbelieving will see in such future signs only what they have seen already, and will remain in their wordliness. When Jerusalem perished, the great type of the world in its destruction, it was thus; and while Christians saw "the abomination of desolation standing where it ought not," and took warning, and fled, the multitude heeded not, were confident, and ate and drank, bought and sold, married and were given in marriage, till their city was encompassed by armies, and they could but remain and die. So it was, says our Lord, before the flood, and before the overthrow of Sodom; and so it would be before the destruction of Jerusalem, and before the end of the world.

What is it that he thus marks and condemns in the conduct of mankind on the eve of such awful changes? It is, surely, not that they eat or drink, or buy or sell, or marry or are given in marriage. These are the natural offices of a life like ours; and without them human society and human existence would close. Of the holiest men, as well as of the most wicked, of Noah and Lot and the truest disciples of Christ it was true as well as of the unbelieving in each generation, that before the tempest of divine judgment burst forth, they ate their daily bread, pursued their business and maintained their domestic and social relations as always before. I remember to have read of a judge who was presiding in a court of justice, when one of those strange seasons of darkness came suddenly on, which have been recorded as "dark days." The new aspect of all things spoke awe to every mind; and the natural thought was uttered by many that peradventure the end of the world might be at hand. With calmness, the judge directed all the proceedings to go on; remarking, that no man could be better employed at the end of the world, than in the way of his duty. There was wisdom, and there may have been piety, in the saying; and although the thought of the approaching end of all things, and of the final judgment, should have a power over the disposition with which every act is performed, it should not prevent or disturb the common acts of daily life, which our Maker has made duties and necessities. Not such could have been the design of our Saviour, when he described the worldliness of those corrupt generations.

This description is as if he had said that they did these things, and did no more. They lived in them: they lived for them: beyond them they thought of nothing. They passed from one of these things to another in willing forgetfulness. In vain for them were all the warnings of prophets, or of the Son of God. In vain might angels descend and walk the earth to gather out and bear to a place of safety, as Lot was borne, all those whose righteous souls mourned for the iniquities which they could not but behold. The crowd of the worldly had no eye or ear or heart for warnings or messengers from heaven. This was their guilt; not that they ate or drank, or bought or sold, or married, or were given in marriage; but that no voice of earnest prayer, no watchful waiting for the Lord, no real concern for his honor or will, no deep thoughts of eternity, sanctified all their business and their lives; but all was only of the earth, earthy.

This worldliness, my brethren, is thus made by our Saviour the characteristic feature in his description of those periods of awful danger. He might have said of the world before the flood, that "the earth was full of violence," and that "every imagination of the thoughts of men's hearts was only evil continually;" for this is said in the book of Genesis. He might have told what is told in that book of the horrid depravity of Sodom, the cry of which went up to heaven; and he might have said, as the sacred writer in the Old Testament has said, that "the men of Sodom were wicked, and sinners before the Lord exceedingly." He might have said of the people of Jerusalem, what at another time he did say, that they had "killed the prophets, and stoned them which were sent unto them," and would slay the Son of the great Lord of the vineyard; or what is related by their own historian Josephus, that before the fall of their city, its streets were filled with unexampled guilt; with murder and plunder, and all their train of horrors. He might have told us, what we know from the book of the Revelation, that before the end of the world, Satan shall be loosed from his prison, and go out to deceive the nations, and gather them in great numbers against the camp of God. Such statements might have displayed the deep guilt and corruption which drew down of old, and must ever draw down, the condemning interposition of Omnipotence. But our

Lord has here intended to exhibit only their worldliness, which, although less guilty than some of the other points of their depravity, yet was, and, while it continues, always must be, the great bar between the mass of men and that only remedy for all their guilt, which mercy might else bestow. The vilest sinner may find pardon and salvation, if he will hear the call of mercy: but worldliness so fills the air with its own sounds and the heart with its own rushing thoughts, that no such still small voice can find entrance.

The principal reason for which our Saviour, both here and elsewhere, so solemnly dwells on the worldliness of men and its peril, is, that this is the most common of all spiritual perils. Most men are worldly. All vicious men are worldly, in addition to their moral vices; and many who are free from the dominion of any one glaring vice, are worldly still. Worldliness, indeed, comprehends the whole circle of those sensual and selfish desires, which fasten themselves to the pomps and vanities of the world; and yet, on the other side, that person would be worldly, and a victim of worldliness, who, without any decided love for one or another of these idols or follies, should simply be satisfied with sitting still, and gazing on the spectacle around him. There may even be much of benevolence, united with such a spirit. Worldliness takes in all who have no aims beyond this world; who seek their portion here, and look on the passing scenes with an engrossing attention. In that circle, then, are the ambitious, who are seeking for themselves worldly distinctions; the covetous, who are wholly intent on that wealth which belongs to this world and can never be carried hence; the voluptuous, who revel in pleasures which are solely of this earth, and of its earthliest composition; the proud, whose eminence is but of the world, but who forget the grave and heaven and hell, in thoughts of that brief eminence. There also are the light and thoughtless, who flutter along through a few days of sunshine, as if this world were nothing else but sunshine. There are the indifferent, who, striving to be satisfied with themselves, have little interest, perhaps, in the things of the surrounding world, but have none beyond. There are all those who have no religious character, no spiritual decision of their own; who only follow the multitude around them, whether to good or evil, but surely in the end to evil. A vast proportion of mankind are embraced within these classes; far more, it is probable, than the slaves of the fierce or the gross appetites which instigate to more conspicuous wickedness. It is not wonderful that our Saviour should so often have held up to view a peril so prevailing; since, if the lusts of the flesh slay their thousands, the lusts of the world slay their ten thousands.

Let me remind you next, that the peril is not in loving too much or enjoying too highly this life and all which it contains. The faithful servant of God draws richer enjoyment from life than all which it yields to the ungodly. The holiest mind may love this earth and all its fair scenes intensely; nay, must love the works of God as we see them here, and the exercise of the powers which he has given, and the society of friends, and all those numberless delights which are perpetually springing up afresh along the path of the cheerful and the thoughtful. It is not in loving or enjoying any thing too much, that the peril lies: it is in loving God and enjoying his presence and his promises, too little. Were but his love supreme in the heart, we might freely eat and drink, and buy and sell, and marry and be given in marriage; freely and fearlessly. "Every creature of God is good, and nothing to be refused, if it be received with thanksgiving; for it is sanctified by the word of God, and prayer." But if the love of God be taken away, every creature may become an idol. Men trifle with the pearl of great price, and far from selling all that they have, that they may buy this, they hold fast all the rest, relinquish this, and thus become the servants, the slaves of a world which, without the blessing of God, can never fulfil its promises of happiness; and which, when it is thus loved more than God, loved while he is not loved, can never have his blessing. "Seek first," he said, "the kingdom of God and his righteousness; and all these things shall be added unto you." The worldliness which he condemns, when it is no more than simple worldliness, simply refuses this commandment. Seek all these things first, it says to itself, and afterwards, the kingdom of God; enjoy the rest as long as may be, and then think of final safety, and find forgiveness. Such a preference has its reward. The cloud of worldliness gathers around the eyes: the current of worldliness wafts on the mind: brighter and better thoughts arise only to be suppressed without delay: there is no time, there is no room for the message of God, until "this night thy soul shall be required of thee," sounds in their astonished ears; or until they drop into the grave, even without that admonition. They have forsaken God, and sought their whole portion in the world; and they have lost all, not because they loved the gifts, but because they disowned the Giver. Here lies the guilt of worldliness. The service of God is rejected, and the service of worldly objects and desires is preferred; and hence the Scriptures denounce covetousness as idolatry. Covetousness is one of the most decided and intense forms of worldliness, but by no means the only one; and all the rest have the same character in this respect, that God is not in the thoughts of the worldly.

The end of all such servitude to the world and its idols, is but too clearly told by all human experience on this side of the grave; and beyond, we know it from divine revelation. For "the world passeth away, and the lust thereof." "All that is in the world, the lust of the flesh, the lust of the eye, and the pride of life, is not of the Father, but of the world," and must pass away. The world which God has made and given us for our abode, and the world which men have made for themselves, in the pursuit of their own lusts and pleasures, are very different. All which in this world remains as it was formed, and all which is sanctified by faith and prayer, may endure or be revived in a better state, or be but exchanged for that which is far better; but what is made the object of idolatry must perish. In each of these memorable instances of which our Lord spoke, and which are past already, destruction came in the midst of all the business and the pleasure in which so many hearts were so rapidly beating. The earth bloomed again after the flood; other cities arose after Sodom was no more; other capitals towered in splendor, when not one stone in Jerusalem was left upon another; but those who had eaten and drunk, and bought and sold, and married and been given in marriage, had all passed on by swift and sudden destruction into the world of judgment. Not by such catastrophes, but by a constant succession of common events, the same divine will is always accomplishing the same issues. When the world has engrossed the few years of life, and has afforded such pleasure as it can, changes come thick upon one another; the grave opens; you pass by again, and the servant of the world is seen no more. But he lived for the world alone; and the world for him is now at an end. He has gone to render his account for the things done in the body; and what account can he render? He must be speechless.

It was in warning, my brethren, that this description of thoughtless worldliness was held up by our Lord Jesus. He bids us take heed of ungodly security and confidence. He points us to those terrible examples. He tells us that such is the course of the world; that such will be our temptation. At the end of the world, at the coming of the Son of Man, he says, the scenes in which men mingle will appear as they did before the flood; as if there could be no approaching dangers, and no eternity at hand. He has told us nothing but what thus far our eyes have seen. We live amongst those who are living thus. All around us are multitudes on whom the thoughts of God, of eternity, of judgment to come, have no power or influence. They eat, they drink, they buy, they sell, they marry, they are given in marriage; and this is all. But Christ would hereby warn us, that this must not be all, if we would die in peace, and live hereafter in joy. There must be a preparation for that life which is beyond this world: there must be an effort to work out our salvation; not by our own power indeed, but through his merit and by the grace of the Holy Ghost. Let such as till now have been but living in this round of earthly occupation and amusement, be warned by the words of our only Saviour. "Ye cannot serve God and Mammon;" nor can ye be lovers of pleasure more than lovers of God, without being dead while you live, dead to the life of heaven. Lift up your hearts above all this stir and noise, this drudgery and machinery of the world, which shuts out the glories of eternity from your inward eye and ear. Well has it been said that the busiest man must find time to die. Consider whether for the sake of life eternal you are not willing to give up whatever the work of a Christian and the hopes of an heir of glory require you to resign. Weigh that question, I beseech you, till you are prepared to decide it deliberately and forever. When it is decided, as I hope it is in many of your hearts, then live by that decision; be pilgrims here; follow not the multitude; use the world as not abusing it; lay up your treasure in heaven, and where your treasure is, there will your heart be also, and there your everlasting home.

SERMON IX.

FREEDOM FROM CAREFULNESS.

Psalm cxxvii. 2.

"IT IS VAIN FOR YOU TO RISE UP EARLY, TO SIT UP LATE, TO EAT THE BREAD OF SORROWS: FOR SO HE GIVETH HIS BELOVED SLEEP."

THE dependence of all temporal blessings upon the gift of the Lord is here the theme of the Psalmist. Except the Lord build the house, in vain is the labour of the builders. Except the Lord keep the city, the watchman goes his round in vain. All toil and anxiety can accomplish nothing without the blessing of him who grants to his own beloved servants, while, trusting in him, they lie down to refreshing and sufficient slumber, that which the ungodly cannot obtain, though they lengthen out the day and shorten the night to the utmost, and eat the bread of carefulness.

There is, then, a certain kind of care which is worse than useless; and there is a certain freedom from care, which is the portion of the servants of God. May he enable us rightly to discern, and joyfully to pursue, the path which he has appointed to be, even here, the path of peace!

Care is universally felt to be the burden of the human lot. "It knocks at the door of the palace;" says the ancient poet; "it sits behind the horseman." Men long for the period when they may have freedom to retire from its oppressive dominion; and they turn back with affectionate regret to the days of their youth, when it was still afar. Who has not wished for a condition of things, were it but possible, in which he might have all which should be needful for his subsistence and comfort, and be left at liberty to apply himself to those pursuits and enjoyments which seem to be best adapted to his own constitution and temper? All this is the language of our nature; of that nature which feels its own fallen state, and loves to imagine to itself something of the better condition which it has lost. Labor, as it is now appointed for man, was not his original portion; much less that heavy solicitude and that inward wear and weariness which now so often accompany and embitter his labor. He desires relief from care, though not, if he is wise, from labor itself, which is the necessary exercise of his powers, and a mighty security against manifold evils.

But notwithstanding the natural and universal wish for freedom from care, there is still an opposite tendency. A certain love of occupation is produced by habit; a certain sense of importance is gratified by being entrusted with many concerns; and we not seldom see those who make almost a boast, and apparently a pleasure, of the very cares at which they sometimes are heard to murmur. But there is still another and a more painful reason for which the cares of this world become even a resource and a satisfaction. A large portion of mankind find it important to such peace of mind as they possess, to avoid all thoughts of eternity. The readiest mode of expelling them, is by filling up the mind with other thoughts of so pressing a character, as to admit no rivals. There are no thoughts which are so urgent and so exclusive as those which the cares of this world involve and introduce; and thus, even these cares are welcome, if they will but banish the admonitions of the world to come. When such men are but relieved from their cares, they become restless, desponding, gloomy. They are haunted by apprehensions, which all reduce themselves to one; the dread of death and of judgment. That is an enemy which can be met face to face, only through the armor of God; through the shield of faith and the sword of the Spirit. To avoid that solemn prospect, they are willing to bear even all the anxieties which a load of cares may inflict; and at which they sometimes betray so much uneasiness.

Undoubtedly, care is a burden; and we welcome it only when we are threatened with the greater burden of idleness, or of fear, or of depression. Occupation, however, is not necessarily care; for, undoubtedly, there is no happiness without habitual occupation. But occupation, without urgent and anxious care, would satisfy the wishes of the human soul, and form its best condition. It is exactly this which the word of God commends to the restless, and promises to the obedient. "The wicked are like the troubled sea, whose waters cast up mire and dirt. There is no peace, saith my God, to the wicked." But "thou wilt keep him in perfect peace, whose mind is staid on thee," are the words of the confiding prophet. While the worldly or vain rise up early, and sit up late, and eat the bread of carefulness and sorrow, God giveth to his beloved, sleep; the quietness of mind which leaves all to him, and can sink at night to rest, "under his own Almighty wings," secure that all will prosper.

But amongst the most dangerous faults are those which succeed in persuading us of their own necessity. When we think we can say, that our folly was the unavoidable result of our condition, remonstrance is almost vain. Even more disastrous, however, it is that the fault should take the name of a virtue. This I apprehend to be at the present time no inconsiderable peril of our own. There is such a pressure on those who are engaged in worldly business; so numerous and so ambitious are the competitors; so frequent are the changes in the state of things to which each business is adapted, and so much do these changes require to be watched and noted, that success is often thought to demand a sleepless vigilance, and a care which will leave no time for other duties. Such care becomes almost a custom; and then it is held a virtue; at least so far, that it may be pleaded as an excuse for the neglect of almost every thing beside. When any man states that his business would suffer, should he relax his attention; that the interests which are committed to his hands will not permit him to turn aside; it is not for others to reply. He pleads duty against duty; and for the time he must be left to his own conscience. He may indeed have come under obligations which now task and tax him to the uttermost; and from which he cannot at once be even partially delivered. But this is an evil; and the evil is tenfold, if such a state is sought and welcomed, and by the young is deemed desirable as well as unavoidable. To be burdened with the cares of the world is then viewed as the portion of the eminent, the honorable and the successful; and, of course, as the road to success, and honor, and eminence.

Do I deny that cares are a necessity, and come along with all usefulness? Do I wish that any should be less useful, or should shun the attendant burden? No; but as the Apostle Paul has said, "I would have you without carefulness;" without needless, wearing, unhappy care; care, which is no attendant on duty, but a mere device for drawing the hearts and minds of men away from God and heaven and real peace. All men have two classes of interests; those of the present life, and those of the life to come. Both demand attention; but the attention which is given to the latter embraces also the former; for godliness has the promise of both worlds alike. Where, however, they seem to come into conflict, the only rule must be, that the weightiest should have the first care and the most; and the eternal interests are always the weightiest. Our Lord has taught us that the cares of this world are amongst the most serious obstacles to that care for the soul, which would secure an inheritance in heaven. His own exhortations against these cares are distinct, strong and numerous. "Take no thought for the morrow," are his words; "take no thought, saying, what shall we eat, or what shall we drink, or wherewithal shall we be clothed?" But if for these things we are not to take thought, then surely not for things far less needful, and only designed to add luxury to comfort, or to secure us, not for the morrow, but for many years, and even to aggrandize our posterity. All of us, then, know that care is a burden; and yet we feel that it is a temptation; we are aware that in our own days it is peculiarly dangerous; and we hear the warnings of our blessed Lord against its influence, and his promises that his servants shall not be subject to its bondage. Let us now consider the manner in which, practically, a Christian should meet and bear the cares which are not to be shunned in his condition, and should shun those which are needless or injurious.

He should begin, my brethren, by overcoming the love of the world, and thus removing the very foundation of all worldliness of practice. Let him set himself down calmly, for once, to that great comparison between the things which are eternal and the things which are temporal. The Lord's day is a fit occasion for such a comparison, and affords a weekly opportunity for renewing it with clearness and at leisure. Let him place in the balance all which he can win by any exertion and with any degree of prosperity, on this side of the grave. Let him carefully exclude even these earthly blessings which no anxiety can defend, and no exertion or worldly success can secure; such as health and a sound mind and the moral and religious character of his children or his beloved friends. These blessings may much depend on his prayers and his faithfulness in duty of the highest order; but assuredly not on his worldly carefulness or worldly labors. Let him then bring before himself this world and the world to come, and make his choice. In one scale let him place all which he can relinquish, by following the commandments of our Saviour. Into the other let him simply cast the sure promise of glory, honor and immortality. Then, having balanced both, he must determine for himself: and every Christian does determine to seek first the kingdom of God and his righteousness. This comparison, distinctly made and often renewed, will lay the true foundation for a just estimate of all earthly solicitude.

Having arrived at this determination, he will sustain and execute it by corresponding habits. The Lord's day will be heartily and entirely devoted to its great purposes of holy rest and of preparation for eternity. His daily devotions, his private and family prayers, will be the most sacred part of his daily business. It will be his steadfast rule to be in the house of God when the word is preached, and the congregation assemble to pray; and he will no more think of refusing these opportunities of refreshing and strengthening his soul, than of neglecting his usual repasts. From the Scriptures he will be constantly drawing that truth which will be the light of his way and the food of his spirit. These will be his great avocations; and while these are the first, he cannot become the slave of worldly anxieties. He cannot be persuaded to give his whole heart and mind to the lower pursuits of earthly advantage; because these habits are constantly leading him back to his higher aim, the prize of his Christian calling.

Under the influence of such feelings and habits, he will not plunge himself, more deeply than is needful, into cares and responsibilities. There are many paths in life; a wise and pious man need not choose exactly that one which leaves least leisure and freedom. In every field of occupation there is a choice between the less and the more perilous ways; between those which promise safety and quietness, and those which tempt to great hazards by the allurements of splendid success. It is probable that almost any business may be carried on without the necessity of comfortless, wearying and mischievous care; but then it must be followed with system, with caution and with forbearance. It is not for me to judge of the limits of necessity in matters quite foreign to the sphere of the Christian pastor. But I can see what is prejudicial to the influence of religion, in one manner of conducting business rather than in another; and it is plain that the more simple, the less entangled, the more regular, the less precarious the transactions of any person are, the easier is it for him to be thoughtful, to be useful, to be generous and to be devout. Complicated concerns, bold adventures, extensive undertakings, hazardous issues, take up the mind, and will not permit it to dwell on the very topic which ought to engage most its noblest faculties. They take up the time, the energy, the activity that might else be turned towards many of those good works, which would bear fruit to the honor of God and to the increase of our own eternal joy. They so involve the question of pecuniary ability, that the man either knows not what is his own and what he is at liberty to give, or cannot use what derives all its real value from its use, or, if he be disposed, has ever a ready excuse for withholding. They engross and distract the mind to such an extent, that private prayer and public worship, and all the means of grace, even if they be not forsaken, are deprived of much of their power, and of almost all their enjoyment. To every Christian who is engaged in business, a just care for his own heart will say, let your transactions, as far as is possible, be simple, direct, and regular. Do not attempt all things. Fasten not upon yourself a needless load, which very probably will result in no temporal advantage, and which will certainly multiply beyond measure the anxieties which, as a Christian, you wish and ought to avoid.

He who would be free from such cares must also cherish within, the habit of leaving all the consequences of his actions in the hands of the Supreme Governor. We cannot make one hair white or black; and every hair of our head is numbered. When the part which was assigned us has been done, nights of restlessness and days of discussion are of no avail. You plan and build, and launch and fit, and man and lade and insure the ship; but when she is once upon the deep, you may as well sleep as toss upon your bed, or watch the winds, or wear out your days with conjectures. It is true that there are many occupations and affairs, in which a constant vigilance is effectual, and is necessary; but even in these there is a limit, beyond which it is useless and vain. If there be any employment which requires perpetual solicitude and the utmost stretch of all the powers at all times, that is an unnatural employment, and one which should be shunned or abandoned, by all who desire peace in this life or in the life to come.

But they who would be without carefulness, must have a cheerful trust and confidence in the Lord, in whose hands are their destinies. Such a trust is what, above all, we need; for with it, no doubt, we shall easily be tranquil and happy, under every vicissitude. The real source of all our care is distrust of God; and the source of this distrust is our consciousness of sin. We do not feel that all is safe with him; and therefore we are anxious. We know that all things work together for good to them that love God; but we doubt whether we are of their number. This is the unhappiness of fallen man, that, even when his mind turns to the power, wisdom and love of his Father in heaven, his heart tells him that he has no longer a just claim upon the protection of all those blessed attributes. The remedy is but one: it is in an humble return, through the mediation of the Son of God, to that state which through sin is lost. This way is open to us: no man cometh to the Father but by him, and whosoever cometh to him, he will in no wise cast out. When you have laid down the burden of your sins at his feet, and have heard with faith the gracious words, "thy sins be forgiven thee," you may cast down also the burden of your cares, and commit your way unto the Lord with the complete assurance that, whatever shall befall you in the paths of his peace, all will be well. Are, then, all true believers the possessors of a perfect freedom from anxieties? Oh, no; else it would not have been necessary that our Lord should have so urged on his faithful disciples, their privilege of taking no thought for the morrow. The true believer is imperfect in this as in every other attainment. He often struggles against a load of anxieties, from which he cannot entirely relieve himself, because his faith is so feeble. Still, in comparison with the worldly, his toil is pleasure, and his sleep is quietness. He does feel, in some measure, that those numerous and blessed promises of the word of God are his, which assures those who trust in him, of all which they can need or ask, since they can ask nothing, and they need nothing, except what shall be for his praise and their own eternal safety and felicity.

"For so he giveth his beloved sleep," while generations of the unbelieving labor through their weary round, returning to the point from which they started. "Vanity of vanities," they cry with Solomon, "all is vanity." Meanwhile a heavenly character has been forming itself in the servant of God, and growing on to its completeness, while he slept as well as when he was awake. He has committed his soul unto One who is able to keep it unto the day of eternal recompense. His own study has been but to be found true to the charge of his great Master. So walking, he is secure. "He that spared not his own Son, but delivered him up for us all, how shall he not with him also freely give us all things?" My friends, do you know nothing of this inward peace? Dare you not trust the love from which you have your life and all its blessings? Seek peace with God through the blood of the atonement; be reconciled to him; and you shall find that everywhere, in life as well as in death, "blessed are all they that put their trust in him."

SERMON X.

CHRISTIAN CONTENTMENT.

Philippians iv. 11.

"I HAVE LEARNED, IN WHATEVER STATE I AM, THEREWITH TO BE CONTENT."

THERE may be minds to which the name of contentment brings but the thought of one of the humbler virtues, of little note in the Christian catalogue. To such the passage may seem a vast descent from the mysteries of redemption, or even from the praises of faith and love, to that lesson which the Apostle Paul here declares that he had learned in the school of Jesus. Yet he describes it as if indeed it were an attainment in which he might deeply rejoice; an attainment which embraced "doing all things through Christ, who strengthened him;" an attainment which was not reached in its perfection by a single effort, in a single moment, but was learned more and more through the whole progress of the soul in holiness. Let it not be imagined, then, that in speaking of such contentment as his own, we are stooping to the walk of mere instruction in the lower rules of temper and of morals. We place before ourselves, rather, in the example of the Apostle, a lofty pre-eminence, of which it may be enough for any of us to say, "not as though I had attained, either were already perfect; but I follow after."

Such Christian contentment, too, is not needed by the poor and the afflicted alone. Many of the evils which most embitter the lives of men, are those which have their seat chiefly in the imagination. Not the less are they to be encountered and overcome; not the less is it sinful to become their desponding and unhappy victim. If those evils which are indeed most severe, are such as fall alike or indiscriminately on all, whatever be their station, then the rich, the exalted, even the prosperous, must study, if they are wise, this lesson which even now, or so soon, they must employ for their own relief. The most discontented persons are by no means those who want most of what we name comforts or abundance. Men are not so much tempted to despondency by the mere absence of earthly benefits, as by causes which lie within themselves, or which may give to their lot some peculiar hue of disappointment. Comparisons create discontent; and comparisons are always easy. The highest of mankind see heights above them. If it were possible, indeed, to gain the whole world, so that no more were left for a wish, yet when the possessor of all reflected, that after a few years he must relinquish all, and take his place with the humblest at the grave and at the bar of God, contentment would be as difficult as ever. We speak, therefore, of an attainment which concerns and invites you all, and not those alone who most need or suffer.

Let me also allude to the exact import of the word which is employed by the Apostle, when he says, that he had learned in every state to be *content*. In the original it has the meaning of "sufficient for myself." Such a translation may suggest to you, indeed, a very opposite quality, and a very odious one; because, in our language, the term "self-sufficient" has become the designation of a wretched arrogance. At the same time, it is plain that, in a noble sense, the wise Christian is sufficient, in himself; in himself, not as distinguished from God, but from the mere power of circumstances; for his own pleasure in prosperity, and for his own comfort in tribulation. Not that he must not rejoice in every outward blessing; not that, especially, the sympathy and the love of kindred souls are not dear to his soul; but that his best strength and joy is from within, from the grace of God within, and there, is maintained in safety. Poor, indeed, my brethren, is that man of whom something like this cannot be said in truth and soberness. Yes, dependent as we are on one another, and on the bounties of Providence, yet has he built the edifice of his happiness upon the sand, who, while Almighty God leaves to him his bodily, mental and moral powers, which form himself, is not, in some sense and in some measure, sufficient for himself. The tempests or the autumnal frosts, to apply an image which may be familiar, will scatter the foliage; but the strong stem and the firm roots should abide unshaken.

But, while this is said, we turn with sacred caution to the source from which the Apostle drew the support of such confidence. He could do all things through Christ that strengthened him; through One who had said that His grace was sufficient for him. That trust alone could avert the charge of boasting. Not one bold word should we dare to utter, of the possibility that in the time of trial we should be found sufficient for ourselves, except it were explained like those of St. Paul, who could elsewhere say, "not that we are sufficient of ourselves to think anything of ourselves; but our sufficiency is of God." It is by the religion of the Gospel that man, the being of to-day, and crushed before the moth, can, as it were, almost defy the changes of time, and can even go with cheerful hope, within the veil of eternity. It is through the disclosures of that Gospel, communicated and unfolded with all their light by the Holy Spirit, that he can learn, in whatsoever state he is, to be content, to find in himself a sufficiency, which is his own, and yet not his own; his own by gift, but not his own by nature.

Let us now proceed to consider those amongst the doctrines of the Gospel, which chiefly create a contentment like that of the Apostle in his imprisonment.

The first is, the universal disposal of a righteous and a gracious Providence. In strictness, this is not merely a doctrine of the Gospel, but of all religion. Our Saviour, however, enforced it by the most beautiful and impressive illustrations. He taught us, too, that the Providence which governs all, is the Providence of a Father; and he dispelled forever the dreams of a supreme government which cares not for actions and fortunes so minute as the minutest of ours. "The very hairs of your head are all numbered." Not a sparrow falls to the ground without your Father. There is scarcely a truth which is clearer to the thoughtful mind than this, that nothing can be beyond the notice or the power of God; and yet there is scarcely a truth which seems harder to be received, in practice, by a part of mankind. They see only themselves and their neighbors, and what they name luck or chance, fortune or accident. If they prosper, it is because they had skill or health, or one or another advantage; and that they had these, is to them only a matter of joy, not of thanksgiving. If they have ill success and trouble, the blame is cast upon friends or enemies, or perhaps even upon themselves; or else it was because they were beset by that strangest of all enemies, misfortune. For misfortune becomes with them almost a real being; and a being, too, whom they may almost hate and revile. To such a man, contentment is no more than submission to that which he cannot avoid. He has done his utmost to brave out the storm, and now he can but sink beneath its fury. Or he has brought it upon himself; and why should he add to its evils by complaints? Not such, however, is the contentment of the Christian. He has learned that the same wise hand on high, gave him the blessings of his lot, gave him the task to employ them well, and gave him the issue, whether it were to be abased or to abound. Calmly and thankfully can he say of all which has befallen him, that, had he all his choice, he could not choose that it should have been otherwise. Will any man, he will ask, wish that the sun might be turned from his course? Will any man desire to govern the clouds of heaven? Will any man long to attempt the task of making the earth fruitful in some other way than that which has been fixed since the creation? Would any man change the whole order of the universe, if he could? Just as little should they wish that the least events of Providence might be beneath their control. Just as little should they desire to add one cubit to their stature, or to gain more than that which justly attends their honest industry, or to lengthen out their days beyond the appointed time. He who governs the universe wisely and kindly, will surely govern with the same wisdom and kindness our little years. He who gave us life, will surely give us food and raiment; and, having these, we may therewith be content.

The second doctrine of the Gospel, which

especially creates a contented spirit, is that which teaches that every state of life is a place of Christian duty. This is plainly taught of the state of suffering, which is named the chastisement of a parent. We know that chastisement has for its very purpose, and for its only purpose, to produce certain tempers which are duties. If this be true of chastisements, it must surely be true of all which is less afflicting, and not worthy of a name so serious. Everywhere he who is at the place which the Providence of God has given him, is at his post, and is set there to do the very duties which surround him and call upon him. If these are the duties of poverty or of sorrow, they are not the less duties; and he ought not to leave them or to wish them undone. The same love must urge him, the same reward must await him, whether he faithfully employ wealth, or faithfully endure want; and the latter is probably an easier task than the former. When we thus feel ourselves engaged, my brethren, in our duty, be it what it may, we cease to repine, we learn to be content. Suppose, under any troubles, that you were told from heaven, that if you would but with patience and cheerfulness bear your burden, you should have an everlasting recompense. Do you believe that you would ever think the labor greater than the prize? Would you ever murmur, with such a crown before you, that too heavy a weight had been laid upon you? You would not, and you could not. But it is surely the same, if contentment be a duty, and if God has promised that no duty shall be done in vain, but shall be followed by blessing and honor in the last judgment. Nor is this all; for greater thoughts than those of reward, even of eternal reward, fill the soul of the believer, and are given him by the Gospel.

Of these is that third doctrine, of a Redeemer, who has loved us and suffered for us. The love of One who has loved us can soar higher than even the hope of heaven. Duty is not only commanded by a divine law, and not only encouraged by divine promises; but it is also warmed with the breath of life by divine mercies. Our Saviour would never have allotted us a task which was either needless or grievous. But all power is given him in heaven and earth. Our present task, with all its duties, is that which he has allotted. Shall we not be content? Shall we not rejoice? To be content is the least which we can ask for ourselves; to be content with that which has seemed wise and good, to the Wisest and the

Best; to him who has told us his love for our souls by the offering of himself a sacrifice for sin. But, besides the sense of his love, the remembrance of his sufferings, sufferings endured for us, creates a contented heart. None of us can venture to compare the sorrows of his own lot with those of that Man of sorrows. If any of us were, as none of us is, so despised and rejected of men, yet none of us has so deserved their praise and love. If any of us were, as none of us is, the heir of such lowliness, in our birth-place or our death, yet none of us has stooped to this lowliness from such a height of glory. It is not hard to conceive of a person who should be happy, in the midst of pain or trouble, at thinking that such was also the life of the Lord our Saviour. But it is hard to conceive of one who should think much of Jesus, and be discontented at these light afflictions, if afflictions they be. There was a time when, in the first love of the Church, men rejoiced to fill up what remained behind of the sufferings of Christ, and met, even with a smile, for his sake, the prospect of torments and of death. We see very often the same support, given by the remembrance of his example, to those who are called to endure long sickness, or great pain, or to lie down and yield up their spirits. Why should we not feel it, then, under lighter trials? Or why should it not lift us far above those causes of discontent, which deserve not the name of trials; envious comparisons between ourselves and our superiors, repining views of our lot, idle fears for the future, impatient struggles against every inconvenience?

A fourth doctrine of the Gospel, which teaches us, in whatever state we are, therewith to be content, is the whole doctrine of an eternal state to come. We can say truly, my brethren, to every discontented person, that he is discontented only because he has not a deep and living faith in this great revelation. It is just as true that the same faith would end the dreams of the proud, and make men of the world moderate in their desires, and open the hands of the covetous. I know that it does not follow, that because we are to live forever, therefore we should neglect to provide for ourselves and our own on earth. It does not make a single duty of our business or station less important. It ought not to drive us into any scorn of society, and its concerns, which are the ordinance of God. Still less ought it to create that kind of spiritual pride, which, boasting of riches beyond the grave, seems thus to answer its own envious thoughts of the prosperity of other men here. But it ought to preserve a constant comparison in the mind between that which is for so little time, and that which is forever, to be held and enjoyed. We well know how to make such comparisons between hours and days, between days and years; why not between years and eternity? It ought to check always the undue wish for some good with which we can easily dispense for a little while; and it is this undue wish which makes discontent. The thought that we are to live forever ought to fix our minds so much upon treasures which cannot be taken away, that we should, as it were, forget our present lot, or at least be only anxious to fill it safely and wisely, and so that we shall not fear the final account. If I am to be happy soon and forever in the joys of heaven, it cannot much avail that I suffer in this brief life. If I am to be wretched, soon and forever, in deserved punishment, it would surely avail little that every desire should now be gratified. But if I am to decide now, whether I shall be thus forever happy or forever wretched, have I not other things to employ my thoughts, than the evils of that lot which it has pleased God to give me, that in it I might work out my salvation? In the one thought of eternity all others are so lost, that we stand amazed, when, turning to the world and to ourselves, we see the power over our happiness, of all which this life can give or can take away.

A fifth doctrine of the Gospel, fatal to discontent, has been omitted, but must not be passed without a mention. It is the doctrine of our sinfulness; the doctrine that we have not deserved the blessings which we taste, and have deserved far greater evils than we suffer. He who is sincere in this confession, cannot but feel that every murmur should die away, or be changed into a thanksgiving. Snatched from the verge of everlasting wo; placed beneath the light of the loving-kindness and tender mercy of God; and called to seek and find, if he will, a crown of heavenly glory, how can he mourn that he has no more?

Thus may we learn, my brethren, from the Gospel, to be content. The thoughts of Providence, of duty, of Christ, of eternity and of sin, need but be seated in our souls; and we must then be much more than contented; we must be peaceful, grateful, happy in unmerited mercies. Learn then of Him who was meek and lowly of heart. In vain should I exhort to such contentment the proud, the worldly, the unconverted, who have none of his spirit. They must be born again. But when you hope that you are learners in the school of Christ, learn there to be content. Lose not your quietness here, and your rest hereafter, through a selfish and an impious dissatisfaction. Build high your everlasting hope upon that rock which is Christ; and amidst blessings even more vast, shall come the sweet calm of a contented mind, enjoying all and fearing nothing.

SERMON XI.

CUTTING OFF THE RIGHT HAND.

St. Mark, ix. 43—48.

"And if thy hand offend thee, cut it off: it is better for thee to enter into life maimed, than having two hands to go into hell, into the fire that never shall be quenched; where their worm dieth not, and the fire is not quenched. And if thy foot offend thee, cut it off: it is better for thee to enter halt into life, than having two feet to be cast into hell, into the fire that never shall be quenched; where their worm dieth not, and the fire is not quenched. And if thine eye offend thee, pluck it out: it is better for thee to enter into the kingdom of God with one eye, than having two eyes to be cast into hell-fire; where their worm dieth not, and the fire is not quenched."

When a declaration is uttered once, twice, thrice, in immediate succession, it demands a most serious notice; for the speaker designs thus to give to his words a twofold or a threefold energy. When such a declaration is made in language, which has plainly been chosen for its force; when images are employed, which are most adapted to startle and alarm; when all is even clothed in such solemn severity, as would be excessive, except where danger is most to be dreaded, and where ill success would be utterly fatal; then we are sure that the truth which answers to the words, is one that cannot safely be passed by, not even for a moment. Nor would such words be spoken of any very remote or very unfrequent peril, while others, nearer and more probable, should be met by a gentler or but a single remonstrance.

The text is a saying of our blessed Saviour. He who had compassion upon all men, and who came to seek and to save the lost, spoke not of the worm that dieth not and the fire that is not quenched, to create a needless terror. He brought not without meaning before his hearers and before us, the painful, dreadful images of such bloody sacrifice, as that of the hand, the foot and the eye, offered by the act of man for his own safety. It was not a slight danger which was shown us by such admonitions. It was not a distant danger which was signified by the threefold repetition of the same piercing command. The hand, the foot, the eye, are the dearest parts of the body, and the most useful instruments of the mind. The right hand and the right eye are, if possible, most precious; and in the Gospel of St. Matthew, these are mentioned in the record of this saying. If either of these offend, and become an occasion of our sin; if it lead us into constant temptation, and threaten to destroy us, it is not to be healed, guarded, devoted to some other employment, but to be cut off at once, and then to be cast away, as if it were a thing abhorred or dreaded, and never more to be approached. Will its absence be supplied by divine interposition? The Saviour answers not to that question; but says, though its absence should not be supplied, though thou shouldest pass on to the tomb, maimed, halt, blind, it is far better thus to enter into life than to preserve every power till the last, and then pass into scenes which are here described, by no general phrase, and in no subdued tone; but as the valley of Tophet, or of Hinnom, which was without Jerusalem, and was known as the horrible place of guilt and death and human sacrifice and dishonored burial. Only, the worm died in the valley of Hinnom, and the fire was quenched, when the remains of the wretches who were laid there, ceased to feed them; but a worm that dieth not, and a fire that is not quenched, are the woes from which our Saviour commands us to flee at whatever cost, of all which is most precious.

If we observe the places in which the text is found, we shall see that it is connected in one instance with a particular class of sins, which sometimes could not be escaped, where they had been habitually indulged, except through a mighty effort; and in the other instance with the vast value of the soul, and the consequent danger of those offences through which the soul must suffer loss. It is plainly a warning, the loudest, the most awakening, that could be uttered, even though it had been uttered but once, but it is a warning uttered three times, against that sin, whatever it be, which does most easily beset us, and which, if it be not resisted, must work our destruction. Such a warning would be quite needless, were there no such peril. Such a warning would scarcely have been given in this manner, were not such a peril frequent. If there be any among you, as probably there may be, who are thus drawn towards the gates of hell by some one chain that must be severed, God grant that such may so hear the warning of his Son, as now to strike the blow!

The hand, the foot, the eye, which must be sacrificed, is that habit which is the closest;

that indulgence which seems to have become a necessity; that feeling which has intertwined itself among the roots of our constant actions. Ours is no heedless adversary. The author of all evil has often mingled his poisons with the cup which is most alluring to the thirsty. He has employed for the ruin of each age and class those very instruments which might most powerfully attract and most firmly retain the victim. Intense is the might of all habit; but when it is fastened to the lust of the flesh, the lust of the eye or the pride of life, it is not strange if the bond should sometimes seem to defy all effort for emancipation. Thus, the theatre of the whole struggle is often reduced in appearance to a single spot. Under the reproaches of conscience and the calls of the Gospel, the heart consents to abandon all beside. Many sins, we will suppose, have always been beheld with aversion. Others have never become seated. Others have yielded to the impulse of better feelings, and have been shaken off with a satisfaction which gave some foretaste of the peace of a quiet conscience. One yet remains; one mighty fortress; and if it shall remain, thence will go forth the dominion by which all may be again subdued. We are not far from the kingdom of God; we approach, and look, and long: and there is but one stone of stumbling in the way; one favorite offence which checks our footsteps. This is probably the state of many; of some, for whom the Christian profession is prevented by one such obstacle; of others, for whom the profession itself has not been hindered, but has afterwards been made powerless. If one such thing be carried closely in the heart within the Church of Christ, it may there spring up in an hour when we think not, take possession of the whole man, and kindle even there a fire that shall not be quenched.

All are familiar with the example of this in the intemperate. Men, otherwise kind, sincere and judicious, are found in the chains of a miserable habit. To compare it with the eye or hand, is indeed degrading; but it has become to them as strong, at least, as a necessity of nature. It is far easier for one of us to omit a daily meal, however urgent our hunger, than for such a one to pass the accustomed draught untasted. The least mental excitement lifts us above the immediate want of bodily food: it rather drives the intemperate man to his fatal relief. He sees, in his calm and thoughtful moments, that the end of these things is death, and that it is rapidly approaching. He perceives that the body, the soul, and every interest of every kind, are not only in danger, but are absolutely ready to be swallowed up by this single indulgence. He strives a little to control it; restrains himself for a time; endeavors not to pass a certain boundary; desires thus not to part with the pleasure, while yet he would shun the danger; and proves by repeated experience, that it is impossible to indulge his appetite at all, and be in safety. Not only the eternal salvation of his soul, but the very preservation of his life, requires him to cast from him forever the cup of his pleasure. If the sacrifice bring pain of body and anxiety of mind; if it enfeeble his frame, and agitate his nerves, and bear him down to the brink of the grave, he must not hesitate. It is for his life; it is for his soul. To save his life, he would give up his right hand to be amputated; to save his soul, he ought to be willing to lay down his life; and is he now to trifle over a mere habit of gratifying his sense of taste or elevating his animal spirits? We know, indeed, that this is not a struggle in which the mind is always victorious; but we know also, that the battle for all which man can prize, is in this instance fought on the narrow ground of drinking or not drinking one beverage, amongst all those that flow at our command.

When St. Paul stood before Felix, the Roman governor, he reasoned of righteousness, temperance and judgment to come. The governor was an unjust and oppressive man, who hoped for a bribe from this very prisoner. But besides this, his wife Drusilla was with him; and Drusilla was also the wife of a neighboring prince, from whom she had torn herself, to be joined to Felix in an unhallowed and adulterous union. The apostle spoke of temperance, which embraces all things that are pure; and we may be sure that he spoke as John the Baptist had spoken at the court of Herod, so that his reasoning was not mistaken. He spoke till Felix trembled; and there was probably a time when conscience said aloud, "Repent, and flee from the wrath to come." We can well imagine that the power which could meet and drive back that blessed impulse, may have been his attachment to the guilty woman at his side. But there was no other safety. She might be as dear to him as his right eye; there might even be in her condition many an appeal to his sympathy or his magnanimity; but the question was before him, between his soul and his passion; and that passion or some other, perhaps not less guilty, prevailed.

A young man of wealth and eminence came

to our Lord, and asked the way of life. He was pointed to the commandments; and he answered, "all these have I kept from my youth." Then said the Saviour, "Sell all that thou hast, and give to the poor, and thou shalt have treasure in heaven." An opportunity was afforded to that young man, such as, with the same distinctness and otherwise in the same manner, was never brought before any other individual. We know that it is in the power of all believers, by diligence in good works, to lay up treasure in heaven; and that the rich may thus furnish for themselves a good foundation. But never was it said to any other person, directly, by Him who knew all the counsels of God and all the hearts of men, that the simple act of parting with all his worldly estate, an act which can be done by writing the name, should secure him a heavenly inheritance. None but our Lord could so discern the thoughts of the heart, as to know that every thing else, in the heart of such an one, was in such suspense, that this single act would be decisive. The young ruler was not, at least was not at that time, equal to the trial. He was very rich; and his wealth was to him as his right hand; he should have cut it off at the word, and he would have been at this hour a bright saint in glory.

These also are examples; but let us come to ourselves. Why can you not lie down to-night with a quiet conscience, and die, if such should be your sudden summons? Because you doubt whether you are in a state of preparation. Why are you not as well prepared at this time as you can hope to be hereafter? Because you hope to possess a firmer confidence in the application of the promises of God to yourself. Why have you not already that firmer confidence? Because you are but too sensible that your heart and your life are not devoted to God in Christian faith and obedience. Why are they not thus devoted? Because there is a struggle within you between the word of God, with conscience and eternity, on one side, and your tastes, habits, inclinations, or present interests, on the other. So far, the answers may be uniform; but undoubtedly there are many who have never thought with sufficient seriousness on the way to the kingdom of God, to have felt the existence of any special obstacle or offence. They remain as they are, because, in truth, they have no inclination to be otherwise. Many others, however, have better wishes; are accustomed to look from time to time, with seriousness, on the things which are eternal; and have asked themselves what change would be required in them, that they might obtain the prize of the Christian calling. Such persons have reflected enough to be prepared to cast some weights aside; but they must often own that there is some sin which easily besets them; some favorite habit or sentiment which they are not yet prepared to relinquish. It comes with them to a distinct alternative; something which is as the right hand or the right eye must be violently removed, or the whole must perish. When, therefore, they are asked, why are ye not with Christ, the true reply must be, that they are offended by the necessity of some such change or sacrifice.

Thus, the love of money is often the evident cause of offence. Many duties might be willingly assumed; many duties appear pleasant or excellent. But the man has learned to prize wealth above all other earthly advantages, and to dread poverty above every evil. His pursuits and aims have all been directed towards the acquisition, the preservation and the increase of his fortune. But nothing is more certain than that a wealthy Christian must be charitable; that, if he be not, the very stewardship which has been assigned peculiarly to him is neglected; and that if he values wealth more than all the benefit which the due use of wealth can yield to his fellow-men, and shuts up the bowels of his compassion from the sufferings of their bodies and the wants of their souls, the love of God is not in him; the eye of the needle cannot be passed; and he must not hope to hear that saying, "Inasmuch as ye have done it unto one of the least of these my brethren, ye have done it unto me." Here, then, the question of salvation is brought to a direct issue. The love of money, so long indulged, is the right eye: it is absolutely required that it should be plucked out; gladly or with pain, the sacrifice must be made; and he must surrender to God all his possessions, to be held hereafter in stewardship; there is no possible escape. Will he do it, or will he shrink? Surely, it is better for him to enter into life as poor as nine-tenths of his fellow-men, than, having all which he holds, or can obtain, to be cast into hell-fire. This is not precisely the question; because he is not called to reduce himself to poverty; but such an one may be assured that it is hard for him to enter into the kingdom of heaven; and that he cannot enter till he has cast aside this sovereign love of wealth, this covetousness, which is idolatry. The struggle may be as hard as he will; it cannot be harder than to cut off the hand, or pluck out the eye; and it must be accomplished, or all is lost.

Thus, also, some are offended by the dread of losing their place in the regard of some portion of mankind. They have lived for honors, for praise or for fame; and perhaps they have embarked all their worldly interests in some vessel that is wafted only by the winds of popular approbation. The mere profession of religion may put an end to the applause of one class of friends; the profession of a true faith will mark a man in other circles as narrow, bigoted, behind the age. The time often comes when he who will preserve a good conscience towards God, must settle it in his mind to relinquish the honors which were already within his reach, and perhaps were even designed for him by those in whose hands is the power to dispense them at their pleasure. So much may the heart have been fixed on expectations like these, that they may be like the right eye with all its delights. Then, it becomes a naked question, which, however hard, cannot be avoided; whether the commandment of God shall be obeyed, at the sacrifice of these expectations. The soul of man is then in his own hands: if he nerve himself to the task, it is well; if not, the Saviour of the world has laid upon him a fearful looking-for of judgment and of fiery indignation; of a worm that dieth not, and a fire that is not quenched.

Sometimes there is a secret, chosen sin, which maintains its hold, amidst a multitude of religious convictions, and gives the fatal offence. Unknown to men, the halting heart preserves within itself the guilty attachment to one transgression, or the firm aversion to one duty. It pauses there habitually: it is determined there to pause. "In all things beside," it secretly says, "I will obey; but here the temptation is too powerful: I might as well pluck out an eye; so deeply is the inclination planted by nature, so strongly is it rooted by custom. Cannot this one practice be indulged? May I not be excused from this one commandment?" Each of you may know for himself whether there dwells in his own bosom such a besetting sin; and whether, if it be so, he is honestly and steadfastly praying for grace to add this victory. Cost what it may, the price must be paid. If but that one point be left, you may push your efforts all around it; and as armies have so often returned from partial conquest, and seen the enemy whom they had heedlessly left behind, gathered again in their strength, to meet them in the midst of their own weariness, and to pour upon them a rapid and a dreadful discomfiture; so that one sin may rise upon you hereafter, and drag you down from your imagined security, and plunge you into shame and everlasting contempt. Be not deceived; but with one vigorous blow in the strength of God, strike off the offending member. It is generally this first blow that decides the issue. When, afterwards, the danger springs up again, it is more easily overcome. And let him that hesitates, remember the awful words of the Son of Man, and so strike.

Words such as these of our Lord, do indeed compel us to feel our condition, with a weight which is oppressive and crushing, till we humble ourselves under the mighty hand of God, and freely yield ourselves to the renewing Spirit. If we could make our responsibility less; if we could justly deem our life and our decision a matter less serious; the pulpit, you may be sure, would seldom be made the scene of useless denunciation; the ambassadors of

Christ would most gladly excuse themselves from inspiring unnecessary alarm. But we cannot place this responsibility more strongly before ourselves than it is placed by the words of our Lord; we cannot present the sacrifice that may be demanded as more severe, nor the result of refusing it, as more tremendous. With every mortal of mature years it must come to this; shall the soul be subjected to the obedience of Christ and of God? Such subjection must be entire, or it is nothing. To withhold the hand, or the foot, or the eye, is to withhold the heart. I know that the doctrine may have a harsh sound; I know that the struggle may seem to be painfully represented; and it is not in all and at all times, that any such struggle has actual existence. The path of early piety is comparatively easy. Many there are who are not thus offended, because they have not fastened upon themselves the iron bondage of evil habit; nor suffered a favorite sin to become as dear as the dearest members of the body. But for those in whom there is such a struggle, the representation is not given by men, but by our Lord Jesus Christ; and once again we must say, it is better to hear of such a conflict, to anticipate it, to meet it, and to come out from it with any loss which is consistent with victory, than having every member perfect, having wealth, honors, the guilty pleasure, the cherished sin, all safe and all enjoyed, to be cast into hell-fire.

SERMON XII.

TAKING UP THE CROSS.

St. Mark, viii. 34.

"AND WHEN HE HAD CALLED THE PEOPLE UNTO HIM, WITH HIS DISCIPLES ALSO, HE SAID UNTO THEM, WHOSOEVER WILL COME AFTER ME, LET HIM DENY HIMSELF, AND TAKE UP HIS CROSS AND FOLLOW ME."

THE first three of the evangelists have all recorded this memorable saying, and its occasion. Our Lord had immediately before announced to his disciples, that he must go to Jerusalem, and suffer many things of the elders, and chief priests, and scribes, and be killed, and be raised again the third day. It is not said that he named the cross, as the instrument of his death; but the subsequent allusion to the cross would thus be understood, since he was to suffer violence, cruelty, and ignominy, and these belonged peculiarly to the punishment of crucifixion. The Apostle Peter, who had just received the promise of the keys of the kingdom of heaven, was offended at this saying, and even began to remonstrate with his Master. But Jesus, in the presence of the disciples, rebuked him with words of piercing and severe kindness. He warned him that it was a thought most hostile to his kingdom, and according well with the designs of Satan, savoring of the things of men, and not of God. For what could have more successfully overthrown the hopes of a world that waited for its redemption, than if the Son of Man could have been tempted to shrink from his great sacrifice? Or, what could more fatally have arrested the establishment of his cause on earth, than if his apostles and his church had learned to nourish the spirit in which Peter had spoken? Our Saviour, therefore, was not satisfied with a private reproof of his erring follower. He turned and looked on his disciples while he uttered it. Then, passing beyond their circle, he called the people unto him; the people who, at that time, attended him in thousands. He had nothing to win from their support. He desired not their service, except for their own salvation: he would not lead them on, under false and worldly hopes; and he embraced this occasion to display to them the most repulsive aspect of the conditions on which alone they could be his disciples. "Whosoever will come after me, let him deny himself, and take up his cross, and follow me."

It is the Saviour who speaks, on the way to his scene of death. He speaks of any man who will come after him; and the preaching of the cross has attained its end, when the hearers follow Christ as he has commanded. I ask your attention, then, to the question, first of all, what is the meaning of taking up the cross? When this shall have been seen, I will endeavor to point out the manner in which each of us is now called to fulfil the requisition. May the love of our Redeemer so arm us, that we may be neither ashamed nor afraid to tread in his footsteps!

The meaning of taking up the cross is, to be ready for suffering. One who was to endure the dreadful pains of crucifixion, was compelled to receive the instrument of his punishment, and to carry it, or a part of it, upon his shoulders, from the place of judgment or imprisonment to the place of execution. So our Saviour bore his cross, till, when he was probably too weary to sustain longer so heavy a burden, it was laid upon Simon of Cyrene. That a man should take up the cross of another person, would be but a toilsome labor: that he should take up his own, would be the sign that he deemed himself about to suffer upon it. To take it up willingly and without constraint, would be to declare himself ready to suffer.

This meaning would have belonged to the phrase, even if our Saviour had not died, or had died by some other instrument. But since the crucifixion of the Lord of glory, the cross has been a consecrated name. It is forever joined with the name of Jesus: it can signify henceforth no sufferings but those which have a Christian character. The mind would be shocked, if a hardened sinner, in his deepest affliction, or most excruciating punishment, were said to be bearing his cross. Those words would be deemed a kind of profanity, or at least a vast perversion of a form of speech of which the meaning had become fixed and holy. Nor has this been accidental: our Saviour foresaw that after his death upon the cross, no other signification would be assigned to his words: he foresaw and he designed it. He spoke of suffering for his sake, in his cause and service, or after his example. To take up our cross is, to declare ourselves ready to suffer as Christians.

The meaning is still further fixed by the other words, "let him deny himself." We deny or renounce ourselves, when we entirely sacrifice our selfish, personal wishes. It is not natural to wish for suffering: every man desires, and cannot but desire, if it be possible, exemption from that which becomes severe. For its own sake, no suffering, however slight, could be welcome. Our own, immediate, natural inclinations must bow themselves to a higher authority or purpose, before any suffering can be cheerfully endured or expected. They must bow themselves to the authority of Christ and to a Christian purpose, before we can cheerfully expect to endure the cross.

To take up the cross, then, is to be ready for suffering in the cause and obedience of a crucified Saviour. He declares that whoever will follow him here in his example, and afterwards to his glory, must be ready for such suffering. The suffering itself is not further explained by his words, except as they allude either in the text or afterwards, to the renunciation of the natural love of repose, of gratification, of gain and of life, when he requires the sacrifice. But whether it be through persecution from without, or painful resistance from within, he has thus imposed, as the universal condition under which men shall enlist in his warfare, that they hold themselves ready for patient endurance. They serve "under this sign."

It is no objection to this meaning, that it might seem inconsistent with many promises of Scripture, or with the representations through which the teachers of the Gospel strive to allure to the ways of pleasantness and peace. The inconsistency, if it existed, would still be only between one portion of Scripture and another; for both these representations are distinctly scriptural. But indeed there is no inconsistency. He at whose birth the angels proclaimed in their songs, "on earth peace, good-will towards men," he was the same who declared that he came not to send peace on earth, but a sword; the same nevertheless who said to his disciples, "peace I leave with you," and parted from them at last with such words of peace and blessing. The Gospel of the grace of God imparts a higher source of action than the mere inclination of nature, and makes men able to receive a happiness even through self-denial. We have often read of martyrs and eminent sufferers for the sake of Christ, who have been refreshed with such joy, that they deemed their tribulation far greater riches to them than all the treasures of Egypt. The single example is sufficient to establish that promises of perfect peace are not at variance with commands to be ready for suffering.

It is, also, no objection, if one should affirm that he sees nothing in the lot of the most faithful Christians, now, or in many other ages, which can be compared, however remotely, with the sorrows of the cross. Our Saviour has not said that his servants shall of necessity encounter the assaults for which they are prepared. The cross may be taken up without a crucifixion. Far be from us the wish to magnify into intolerable evils, when they are endured for our religion, the inconveniences which multitudes endure in every cause, and for every end. But sufficiently often has the Christian passed through even the fires of persecution, to require that, when the offers of the Saviour are proclaimed, the possibility of even such suffering should be a distinct portion of the prospect. By the great goodness of our God, we live in times of repose, and the religion of the Gospel is honored and sustained. But even now, who could rely upon the perseverance of one who should not have counted the cost, and reckoned in it the hazard of standing amidst many opposers, and, of course, the hazard of some suffering for Christ's sake? It would never be safe, to venture forth upon the path to the kingdom of God, without a readiness to endure hardness. Even many, for whom all would seem to have been most easy and pleasing, would yet confess, if all the secrets of their thoughts and lives were revealed, that, when they endeavored to seek first the one thing which is needful, they were constrained to be made like their Saviour in some one of the features of his passion, though it were but in the coldness of those whom they would gladly have honored and gratified. So general is the original aversion from seriousness in piety. So little does the condition of any age supersede the warning of our Saviour.

The meaning, therefore, of taking up the cross, is, a readiness to endure suffering for the sake of Christ and his kingdom. This meaning we have also seen to be weakened by no objection, drawn from the promises of Scripture or from the actual state of mankind. But such a readiness is not a mere disposition of the mind which cannot be tested, as if a man should declare himself ready to perform some great act of magnanimity or love, which could never be demanded at his hands. It has its constant tests; tests less severe than those for which a Christian ought to be prepared; but tests which, for that very reason, may be more decisive.

The assertion might be made, that he has not the affection of a parent, who would not lay down his life for his children. Our illustration is not dependent upon the truth of this assertion. But if it were allowed and believed by any parent to be true, he could not afford to himself or to others the proof or the presumption that he possessed such affection, through the avowal or the determination that he would lay down his life when the sacrifice should be demanded. If, in his daily watchfulness and kindness, he gave the tokens of a more common affection, they would avail much more. In the same manner our Lord has said, and his words are truth, that, except a man take up his cross, be ready to endure suffering for the sake of the kingdom of God, he cannot be his disciple. It is not enough, and it is not to be desired that, in imagination, we should bring before ourselves the strong anguish of excruciating tortures endured in that cause, and in imagination triumph over them. If we are ready for suffering, the readiness, at least, will reveal itself, where the suffering may scarcely deserve that name. In the passage of St. Luke, which corresponds with the text, the words of our Saviour are expressive of this: "Let him deny himself, and take up his cross *daily*, and follow me." The cross is thus brought to our doors, to our daily walk; not to be endured in its pains, but to be borne in sign of readiness. Let us proceed, therefore, to ask, how is the cross to be taken up and borne by each of us? How is our readiness to suffer for Christ's sake to be declared and tried?

In the first place, my brethren, by the steadfast profession of faith in his name and Gospel. He has admonished us and all men, that openly to confess him before men is a duty that cannot be absent from a right hope in his redemption. Whosoever shall be ashamed to fulfil it, of him shall the Son of Man be ashamed, when he shall come in the glory of his Father. In prosperity as faithfully as in tribulation; in tribulation as firmly as in prosperity, the Christian must bear, in his profession, the sign of the cross. When he seems to himself but a single, feeble champion, whose aid will not be missed, he must not let it be unknown, on which side in the conflict he is found. When the standard seems to waver, and he can but desert it or die in its defence, he must not desert it. In the most peaceful times, this duty must not be held too easy to be important: in the most perilous, it must not be held too hard to be done. I name it, then, a taking up the cross, when, by any person, the name of Jesus is publicly professed, through an habitual communion with his Church in all its holy ordinances. If such a one were called to endure suffering, his very profession, the cross which he had borne, would remind him of his obligation, and upbraid him if he chose rather his safety and his ease. He, on the other hand, who has given no such pledge, has not taken up the cross, and may renounce it without inconsistency, but not without condemnation. Tell me not that a religious profession attracts the respect, rather than the scorn or opposition of men; or tell it me from your experience. Tell me not that it would be such a happiness to embrace it, but for peculiar fears of unworthiness, that the reproach or ridicule of the wicked would be held as nothing; or tell it me still from your experience. Till then, you may believe it, indeed; and you may be deceived. I speak not of the vicious or the thoughtless, but of those who have meditated on that sacred duty, and still defer its performance. Is it not chiefly because, by that profession, you would engage yourselves under weightier and holier promises and pledges than any which you have taken upon you; promises and pledges to walk answerably to a Christian calling? You may be afraid that you should violate and dishonor your covenant. You may dread the censure of those who might mark your deficiencies. You may be overawed by the greatness of the work, and the solemnity of the sanctions. You may be really unprepared to take a part so decided, and a name so holy. I am not exhorting a double-minded man to acts for which he has no heart. I would not willingly persuade a single soul to a hypocritical or an inconsiderate profession. Stay till your choice is made; but be assured that, under whatever form this dread or unwillingness exists, it is a dread or an unwillingness to take up the cross. It is nothing but the cross from which you shrink. He who is unprepared for a solemn profession of his faith in Christ, is unprepared for suffering in his cause; even the suffering which may befall a Christian now.

In the second place, the cross must be taken up, by separation from the world. The restraints of our duty must not be disguised through the plea, that no innocent pleasures are forbidden by the law of Christ. None are, indeed, forbidden, which would be innocent at the time and place at which they are forbidden. But the world is filled with the means of enjoyment. Some of them are vile and guilty, and yet are pleasant to the eye and the taste. All of them, however sweet and pure and excellent, are yet safe only when they are employed in obedience to some higher command than that of the inclination which bids us enjoy them. Why should the candidate for a Christian recompense be told that he need relinquish no pleasure? He must relinquish many. If they cease to be pleasures, when they would be dangers, the greater is his happiness; but this is no part of the promise by which he is encouraged in his duty. The very spirit of the world is that of seeking to gather around ourselves the materials of enjoyment here, afar from heaven. It will admit so much influence from religion, as may favor its own end, but it admits no more. The world, in the scriptural sense, consists of those men who are living for that end alone, and of those things which are only subservient to that end. A Christian has a higher aim, and must separate himself from these. He must be crucified to the world. So far as it strives not against his heavenly character, he may use it, as not abusing it. But he must bear the cross, by holding himself ready to lay aside any benefits or enjoyments, so soon as his more exalted vocation shall command. Even while he tastes them, his heart must not be upon them. It must be his chief endeavor not to enlarge his possessions, but, as a wise steward, to employ for good that which he may possess or acquire. He must turn from the pursuit of mere gratification, in society or in study, and seek that every hour may bring, in some manner, its contribution to his own improvement, in soul and mind; and to his fitness for his duty and for a blessed destiny. The conduct which proceeds from such efforts will withdraw him from many scenes and occupations in which he could doubtless find enjoyment, but for which he has not leisure. A successful missionary in a heathen land was invited, after an absence of many years, to revisit his country. He wrote in reply, that it would be to him indeed an exquisite joy to see once more the faces of his early friends, and talk of all which had passed; but that surrounded by such a sphere of duties, he must reserve that joy till they should meet in a better country. It is in this spirit that we ought to be prepared to pass by innocent, and even praiseworthy pleasures. There is no time for half of them here. God has set before us a higher prize; and it is a part of our trial to choose between the less and the greater, the temporal and the eternal. That which is indeed excellent, may become fatal, if it enter into rivalship with that which is first of all to be sought, the kingdom of God and his righteousness. We may give to study the hours that should be given to divine worship. We may be rejoicing in the company of prosperous friends, when we should be at the bedside of the sick and dying. We may lavish in tasteful embellishments the money which ought to have made glad the widow and the fatherless, or to have sustained the means of grace amongst them that perish for lack of knowledge. We may plunge ourselves, with all our powers, into the successive currents of popular excitement, till no feeling is left, to be moved by the voice that speaketh from heaven. Such pleasures, then, must be enjoyed with chastened affections; affections crucified, or fixed to the cross. Thus is that cross taken up, through a reasonable and religious separation from the world and its sovereign, earthly desires.

In the third place, the cross is taken up, and taken up daily, through the constant subjection of self-will. There is always a suffering, however slight, in the surrender of our own first choice, until this is rendered easy by some superior principle, which is chosen in preference. That principle is formed by the Gospel, and especially by the grateful love which it inspires for the character, example and propitiatory sufferings of the Redeemer. He endured the cross, not because he did not feel every one of its pains and indignities in their keenest anguish, but because his love for the souls of men, and his anticipation of the joy that was set before him, triumphed over all. The cross, thus endured, is made the sign of Christian self-denial. It becomes an established rule of daily duty, that we must show ourselves ready for that kind of suffering which is felt where our own previous wishes, of whatever nature, are relinquished for the name of Christ, and for the happiness of our brethren. Do you ask, whether you could, for the sake of your Lord, forsake father and mother, and wife and children, and houses and lands, to go with him, if need were, to imprisonment and death? Ask rather, whether you can suppress, for his sake, the hourly impatience, the words of irritation, the desire of honor, the love of ease, the unholy gloom, the censorious reproach, the strenuous maintenance of your claims, the disposition to look only on your own things, not on the things of others? For he who proves that, in the daily government of his acts, the will and precept of Christ can place in constant subjection every rising wish and preference, takes up his cross, denies himself, and has the same spirit in which martyrs have gone to their crowns.

Finally, the cross is taken up, and in some sense endured, too, through the patient, pious endurance of sorrows. It may be the lot of few to suffer many things for the sake of the cause of Christ; but all must suffer. The spirit in which affliction is borne, may exalt it into a kind of participation in his sorrows, having a part in the same consolations, and the same reward. The worldly sufferer is like the impenitent malefactor, who died indeed upon a cross, but it was only a cross of shame and punishment. The Christian sufferer is like the other malefactor, whose cross acquired a likeness to that of Jesus, and became a pledge of future glory. By the habitual remembrance of our true condition here, by humble acquiescence in the sufferings which must be to come, and by the meek endurance of those sufferings when they arrive, we show ourselves ready to be conformed to the image of Christ, and to be made partakers of his cross.

And now, by what argument shall you be persuaded thus to deny yourselves, and become, in readiness for every suffering which truth and duty may impose, the followers of the Lord our Saviour? It would seem almost irreverent to name any other motive for taking up the cross, than those which come from the cross itself. Remember, how dreadful beyond all thought had been the misery of our souls, if, once stained with guilt, they had been left without the interposition of mercy. Think on the wonders of redemption, on the cup which the Lord received from his heavenly Father to drink, which, if it had been possible, had been passed by; the cup of supernatural agony, so patiently exhausted for man. Look on the cross of Christ, as the sole refuge of your spirits, and remember how surely, in the hour of death and in the day of judgment, your hope will fix itself there, if any where, in heaven or earth. Will you not take up this hallowed cross, by the open, steadfast profession of your faith; and if that be already begun, by separation also, from the pomps and vanities, the idle or untimely or excessive or insufficient pleasures of the world; by the daily subjugation of your own wishes to the will and word of the Lord; and by the patient endurance of your appointed portion of sorrows? How cheerfully will this task be undertaken, if the love of Christ constrain us!

SERMON XIII.

CHRISTIAN DUTY TO FRIENDS.

St. John, i. 41.

"He first findeth his own brother Simon, and saith unto him, We have found the Messiah."

John the Baptist, on a certain day, directed two of his disciples to the Lamb of God who taketh away the sins of the world. He pointed to our Saviour as he passed by, so that the two knew the person of Jesus, and followed at once to his abode. There they remained, and listened to his words, till they were satisfied that they had found the Messiah.

One of these disciples was the future Apostle St. Andrew. His first impulse was now to seek his brother Simon, afterwards named Peter, and communicate to him, the amazing, joyful discovery. They went together to Christ; and thenceforth they travelled together as Christians. Brethren by birth, brethren in faith, brethren in the apostleship, brethren in martyrdom; they are now brethren also in the joy and glory of their Lord, and they shall sit upon two of the twelve thrones, which shall be set for the judgment of the tribes of Israel.

The impulse which Andrew obeyed with such blessed results, was that of natural affection. Natural affection *commonly* coincides with the highest duty. The man who does not love his kindred, cannot much love any other person, and has already passed into an unnatural selfishness, on which no religious character can be engrafted. "He that loveth not his brother, whom he hath seen, how can he love God, whom he hath not seen?" The affectionate heart is the soil that will bring forth fruit, through the blessed seed of the Gospel. We cannot advance a step in religion, without true love; and we cannot have love, unless it be first toward those whom nature has made dear, and whom God has enjoined us first of all, to honor and to cherish. When he commands us to love as brethren; when he assures us that we are all brethren, because we are his offspring; he makes the love which we owe to our nearest relatives, to brothers and parents, the example and standard of Christian benevolence. The former is presupposed; and it is intimated that charity cannot go beyond the affection which is due from brother to brother. Thus are the natural feelings consecrated by the Gospel; and we now propose to consider the very delicate but very sacred subject, of the duty of those who believe in the Lord Jesus and hope for heaven, toward those amongst their dearest friends, who as yet are not partakers of their faith and hope. May the God of love guide us, and fill us with all gentleness and tenderness, all faithfulness and truth!

It is an inestimable mercy, that, under the constitution of our nature, and under the influence of our domestic relations, persons of the same family, so often and so easily become united in religion. The examples in the New Testament are very numerous. This of Andrew and Peter is one; you may remember those of the families of Lazarus of Bethany, of Mary the mother of Mark, of Alpheus, of Stephanas, of Lydia, of Onesiphorus; that of the house of Zebedee is another; and still another is that of the kindred of our Lord, at first unbelieving in part, but afterwards his followers. There has never been a Christian community, in which such examples were not numerous; and the Gospel has been propagated at first, very much through the intercourse of the members of families. This is as much the ordinance and institution of God for this purpose, as is the existence of the church and the ministry. What other opportunities can be compared with those which are afforded by constant sojourn beneath the same roof, by daily meeting at the same board, by almost hourly conversation, by perpetual association, side by side? What other influence can be so uninterrupted, so mighty, and so tender? Where can motives so powerful be always in operation? Who can care for the salvation of a child, if not his Christian parents; who for that of a parent, if not his Christian child? Whom shall the converted Andrew first seek, if not his own brother Simon? Whom shall the pious wife endeavor to win by her pure conversation, if not her unbelieving husband? All causes and all commands unite to constrain the endeavors, which bring so often so rich a return of blessing.

Many there are in every Christian assembly, who have within their heart, no wish so warm and deep, as that some very dear friends, the objects of their tenderest and holiest love, should share with them the blessed, the distinct, well-founded hope of life everlasting. Every Christian will respond to this feeling; and in some it is most anxious and intense. Scarcely can it be mentioned without such a sense of the extreme delicacy of the feelings and relations with which it is connected, as almost imposes silence. Let us not allude to these more fully; but let us suppose, what I am sure we are warranted in supposing, that any one who has the spirit of Christ, would rather lay down his own life, with the peace of God and the sure hope of glory in his heart, than that the soul of parent or child, consort or brother or sister, or near and dear associate, should be lost. To those who thus feel, let us speak of the means through which they are permitted to seek for all whom they love, what they most prize for themselves.

They can and they must offer the unceasing sacrifice of their intercessions. Those who can do no more, can pray; and those who can do much more, can add their prayers, without which all else may be unavailing. The privilege of prayer for our friends, is one which may be estimated when we think how desolate would be our lot, were it denied. If we were told by the word of God, that each of us must work out his own salvation, and answer for himself alone; that it would be a sinful presumption to approach the throne of grace with any petition, even for the dearest brother; hard indeed might it be to submit; and bitterly might we long for some indulgence of our love, for some glimpse of favor towards the warm desire of our souls that they might be saved. But now the permission is not withheld; the divine charge to us is, "in every thing, by prayer and supplication, to let our requests be made known unto God;" and this charge covers all which we can wish to ask for our friends and brethren. We go to the mercy seat, to join our prayers with theirs, if they are there; and if they are absent, to offer ours so much the more fervently in intercession. It is much to be permitted to pray, even were there no assurance of an answer; but we do not pray without a promise. The general promise includes these prayers as well as those which go up for ourselves; "ask, and ye shall receive; knock, and it shall be opened unto you." Not for himself, but for his servant, the believing centurion besought our Lord and was accepted. All the instances in which the sick were brought to Christ, and two of those in which he raised the dead, were instances of a gracious reply to the prayer of believing friends. These prayers were presented for bodily healing and earthly life; but none can doubt that much more acceptable, and as readily granted, are those which ask for spiritual grace and life eternal. If from the result we can at any time prove that prayers have been answered, the proof is no where more clear than in prayers for the inward and everlasting gain of others. How many thousands of religious parents have prayed without ceasing for their children, and have seen them, one by one, all coming to take their places amongst the servants of God, and rejoicing in the hope of pardon and of glory! How often have such prayers followed even those who have wandered far from the truth, and seemed hopelessly lost, and who yet, late but not too late, have returned like prodigals. It would be entering into the secret history of hearts, to tell how a single devoted friend has sometimes asked for some friend who had his warmest sympathy and affection, the gift of that one thing which was lacking; has asked it long and without weariness; and at length has seen, with joy unspeakable, the signs of an humble and believing heart, and has been ready to cry, "Lord, now lettest thou thy servant depart in peace!" Let every Christian, encouraged by such examples, persevere in intercessory prayer. All have dear friends; almost all have such friends, who are as yet without godliness. Pray for them, in proportion as they are near to your souls; in proportion as you wish to be with them in joy forever. Pray for them even until you obtain your request, or till death shuts up the scene of probation. There is no limit to the efficacy of such prayer, except this, that every responsible creature must have the power to reject the grace of God, and, if he reject it, must perish. Not absolutely, therefore, can it be said that the purpose for which we pray will be attained; but we may be sure that such grace will be given as shall awaken the conscience, present the strongest motives, cherish every rising desire, and assist every effort to reach salvation. This is enough; more we cannot even ask for ourselves; for, it must rest with us at last to make our salvation impossible, if we cling to iniquity. For all which God is accustomed to bestow, we may confidently pray; assured that "the acceptable, fervent prayer of a righteous man availeth much." Try all its powers, O Christian, in behalf of those you most deeply love, and you shall have your reward.

To prayer we must be prepared to add direct exertion. Perhaps, it is in this that most of us are most deficient. We do not enough exhibit to our friends, the solicitude which we really feel for their eternal welfare; and they may imagine that we feel it not. I know the many difficulties which prevent what our hearts are often burning to perform. There are limits in all social intercourse which we are not permitted to pass; nor can our best counsels be repeated with very great frequency, lest they become wearisome and repulsive. We owe a respect to age, to station, and to various relations which forbid us to intrude unasked advice, much more to venture reproof that would but irritate. Days, months and years glide on; we meet, we converse, we aid one another, we fulfil all the various offices of life; but on the great end of all, we are silent. Then, sickness steals in, and there is very little time or opportunity to say, what should long since have been said; and death arrives, and it is unsaid still. How often has this been the experience of families and of friends! How many a time, has it been too late the source of bitter regret, that at no moment had the Christian ever distinctly spoken as Andrew spoke to Simon; "we have found the Messiah; come and see!"

With children, the task is easy. They expect counsel, instruction and assistance; and they so need it at every step and in all things, that they will never be surprised at receiving it for their everlasting advantage. They may well be surprised should it not be offered. Who shall guide them, if not their parents? Who, if not their Christian parents, should show them the way to heaven, and press them to walk in it from day to day? There is no obstacle, except the dread of wearying them with too much of admonition. But this need not be much feared, if it always proceed from an affectionate heart, which is ever giving proofs, that in all things it serves their happiness.

With older friends, undoubtedly there is need of greater caution. We have not the same social rights, nor have they the same submissive readiness to listen. Still, there are times for all things; and there is a time for conversation, yes, for frequent conversation, with our dearest friends, on interests of unparalleled importance; the only interests, which after a little while will remain to them, or to ourselves. There ought to be nothing secret between us in these concerns, beyond that which is to be told to God alone. But, how frequent are the occasions on which we might speak of heavenly things, had we but the heart and the tongue! Are they not the natural subject of discourse on every Lord's day, and under every serious dispensation of Providence, and indeed under all the constant mercies which make up our daily life? When is it unreasonable to speak that which, in one manner or in another, may conduce to edification and to godliness? What we need is a frank and open way of conversing upon religious things as naturally as upon all others. Let us put away this false fear and absurd restraint; and think, and speak, and act, as beings who are to live forever, and who wish to live together in eternal joy. There should be, then, and there will be times, when a friend can speak to the heart ot a friend. That which from the pulpit is the language of doctrine and exhortation, becomes in such private discourse, the language of experience and persuasion. They who are ever ready to speak will not lack the opportunity. But if it seem not to come, let it rather be sought, let it rather be created, than suffer one who is near and dear, to live and die, without some effort to bring him to endless glory.

Many will tell me, however, and tell me truly, that words without deeds are of little avail; and that words contradicted by the life, are worse than worthless. We cannot conduct our brother to Christ, except we go with him; we cannot go to our Redeemer, without that love and humble faith which are the gift of God, and which he never withholds from those who desire and pray to find rest unto their souls. If you would have courage to speak of religion, and power to speak of it with success, let your life be that of a blameless Christian; and for this, your faith must repose constantly and warmly on the promises of your heavenly Father. You must draw nigh to him through Christ; you must live in communion with him, by prayer and thanksgiving; you must be watchful, careful, consistent, conscientious; you must take heed that you grieve not the Holy Spirit of God, whereby you are sealed unto the day of redemption.

If we converse with men as we find them, we shall observe how much, how far too much indeed, their views of religion are drawn from the actual examples with which they have been familiar. One will tell you, that his parents were persons of piety; that he can never doubt the reality of that religion which governed them; and that he is sure that, if there be a heaven, they must be its inhabitants. Another will say that his youth was thrown amongst those who professed a faith which was rigid and condemning, and who shunned many innocent enjoyments, but were selfish, covetous, unfeeling and utterly without Christian kindness; and that he has never been able to recover from the unfavorable impressions of his early days. They will point you to certain professors of religion, and will say, "those are the stumbling blocks in our way; through their worldliness, their pride, their avarice, and their folly; unless we can be better Christians than they, we will undertake nothing." They will tell you, perhaps, of others whose daily life is to them a living exhibition and proof of the gospel; whose charity, meekness, integrity, faithfulness, consistency and humility are evident fruits of another spirit than that which fills the children of this world. I said that the views of men are far *too much* drawn from actual examples. They ought to look higher, to the one great Example; to Him who did no sin, and to His word with all its spotless pureness and its unmingled truth; for, all actual examples must be most imperfect, and many will lead astray. Yet, my Christian friends, we must meet the demand which our fellow men make upon us; it may be unjust to themselves, but it asks from us no more than what is strictly just, and our bounden duty. Our blessed Lord has told us how terrible a woe shall fall upon that man by whom the offence cometh; while it is the crowning excellence of that exceeding great reward which awaits the faithful and upright man, that he shall not only save himself, but those who are with him; that the Lord "showeth mercy unto thousands in them that love him, and keep his commandments."

For the sake of your beloved friends, therefore, adorn your calling. Commend it by your upright and pure example. Probably no arguments will have power without this; this may be mighty without others; and if you desire that your prayers should be answered, you must add to them the only sufficient proof to yourselves, of their sincerity and fervor; the proof afforded by a truly religious life. Let this motive prevail with you, in all your duties; fastening itself to your fear of God, and your love for your blessed Redeemer. Anticipate the future; anticipate the day when the book of life shall be unrolled, and all the web of causes and of consequences shall be displayed; and every man shall receive according as his work shall be. The story of this life will be then remembered, as at evening we recall some adventure of the morning; but more clearly than the minutest map, more fully than the exactest narrative, will it all lie before your eyes. You will perceive the chain which linked together the smallest events and the greatest;

each man and all his race; the successive days and eternity. If you have so lived that you have drawn many others to live to God; so that you have come to your everlasting joys accompanied by a train of dear friends, whose friendship here you can remember even there with ever new delight; most blessed may you be, even amongst the blessed.

SERMON XIV.

CHRISTIAN CHARITY.

1 Corinthians, xiii. 13.

"THE GREATEST OF THESE IS CHARITY."

IF every mortal were permitted to select and claim that possession which he might esteem most precious of all, many, no doubt, and perhaps most, would choose a cheerful, established *hope* of happiness after death. None are entirely without solicitude for that interminable future; and all can appreciate the lightness of heart with which the present hour must be enjoyed or endured, when all is bright beyond. How often is religion regarded merely as the giver of hope! How many think of the Gospel solely as that power, which sheds consolation over the troubled soul, and forms, from the chamber of death, the porch of immortality!

A Christian, however, acquainted by experience with the blessedness of hope, yet fixing his eye more on the actual certainty, than on the pleasing confidence which it might inspire, would very probably see a superior dignity in *faith.* It is faith through which the sinner is justified. Faith without hope would still be secure, while hope without faith, would prove itself the most ensnaring delusion. "He that believeth, is passed from death unto life." Faith overcometh the world: faith can accomplish mighty wonders; the prayer of faith availeth much on high; the life of the just is a life of faith; and the righteousness of God is revealed from faith to faith. The supplication of the servant of Christ is daily ascending, for a firmer, a livelier, a more victorious faith; for he is assured that he owes to the weakness of his faith the inconsistencies which he must deplore in his life; and that, if he can but walk as seeing those things which are invisible, he will tread a safe and an exalted way.

Yet the Apostle Paul, when he has named together the three essential graces of true religion, declares that the greatest of these is *charity;* and thus ascribes to it some high superiority over the hope which men desire, and over the faith which Christians value. Nor is it enough to say, as is sometimes said, that charity remains in the heavenly state, when faith is exchanged for sight, and hope is lost in enjoyment. Who knows that neither faith nor hope can be exercised in Paradise or amongst the angels? The thought, indeed, which it is designed to express when this is said, is probably less concerned with the duration of either, than with their essential relation to each other. It is not so much that faith and hope must cease while love abides, as rather that faith and hope are both of the nature of means; have both a reference to something still beyond; while love may be deemed an end, the actual union of the spirit with God. Love is the fulfilling of the law; but the law could fix no rule except that of perfectness; therefore love must be the highest and most perfect state of such a being as man. But the will of God is to be done on earth as it is done in heaven; man, made a little lower than the angels, is made in the image of God; and that which forms the perfectness of his state, must be the divine nature, and the nature of all pure and sinless beings. This, too, is affirmed by the Scripture; for "God is love."

But whatever may be the exact character of the superiority of love, the superiority itself is asserted without a qualification; and not its superiority alone. Its supreme necessity is declared in language which casts faith itself, so far as faith might be without love, and casts works and sacrifices, the noblest and the most determined, so far as these might be without springing from love, into obscurity and worthlessness. "Though I have all faith, so that I could remove mountains, and though I bestow all my goods to feed the poor, and though I give my body to be burned, and have not charity, it profiteth me nothing." These are solemn words; more solemn, perhaps, than they seem, familiar as they are to our ears and thoughts. For some cause, whatever it be, they are rather admired for the beauty of the doctrine, than weighed with a just conviction of its awful seriousness. For some cause, whatever it be, men are not ready to suspect themselves, as wanting the spirit of Christian charity. They lament the slowness of their faith, the weakness of their hope, the slightness of their repentance, the coldness of their devotions; but less readily deplore the deficiency of their charity towards mankind. If they are governed, as they trust, by their knowledge of the faith of the Gospel, and if their path is illuminated by the rays of a distant hope, they seem but too often to assume that love cannot be absent. To intimate that possibility would perhaps startle many a person, as if he awoke from a dream, while, notwithstanding, it might be difficult to recognize in his character, the picture which has been drawn in this thirteenth chapter of the first Epistle to the Corinthians. But when you remember that, should it indeed be absent, all the rest is so vain, so heartless, such sounding brass and tinklings of the cymbal, you must believe it worthy of your most earnest examination, whether your religion is that which profiteth, that which has put on charity, the bond of peace and perfectness.

In aiding this examination, we must commence with a nearer view of the grace which is upheld as so indispensable and so exalted. I need not, perhaps, to remind you, that there is no distinction between charity and love, in the original language of the New Testament. I may remark, however, with propriety, that the distinction in the English language between the two words, a distinction by which the translators seem to have been guided, is, that love denotes rather the feeling and principle, as existing within; charity, as both existing within, and manifested in the outward life; that love, also, may be directed towards God or man, while charity is more strictly employed of our love to one another. It is true, and a truth of deep import, that the love of God cannot glow, without expanding itself towards all whom He has loved; and that the love of man is not Christian charity, except it be one with the love of a common Father in heaven. But it is also true, that where charity, under that name, is extolled and urged in the Scriptures, as in the chapter before us, it is clearly described in its exercise towards our brethren. Each feature of the portrait will confirm this representation.

"Charity suffereth long, and is kind." The first impulse of the human heart, on the reception of a wrong, is to assert its right, and to resent the injury. Amidst the occurrences of every day, the inclination to resentment has constant occasions; and our trial is chiefly with the less amongst these occasions, not with the greater. In almost every transaction, some fault has been committed by some person. To suffer long where indeed there is no blame; to preserve ourselves from impatience, when indignation could find no object; even this is no inconsiderable triumph. But to preserve the same unbroken kindness where blame is justly deserved; to reprove only when it will be beneficial, and only because it will be beneficial; to suffer again and again, till seventy times seven, the waywardness of the thoughtless, the wavering purposes of the fickle, the real mischief inflicted by criminal carelessness, nay, the insulting reproach or contempt which are most unmerited and cruel; to suffer long, towards those whom we neither dread nor are bound to revere, those whom we have perhaps the authority to control, perhaps the power to punish; this is the charity of the Gospel. It asks neither insensibility nor weakness; but only the spirit of Him who is long-suffering and slow to anger, forgiving iniquity, and transgression and sin, and desiring not the death of the sinner. It forbids impatience and vexation at the little disappointments wrought by the negligence of others; strict requisitions of compensation for injury, intentional or unintentional; a hard and rigid temper towards children and dependents; indulgence of occasional irritability, however transient; and even severity of condemnation towards undeniable guilt. Are we quite sure that we possess this heavenly grace? Can we distinguish it by that best test, our own experience, from that indolent disposition, which has always the air of an indiscriminate kindness, not because it suffers long, but because, from its indifference to means and ends, to good or evil, it suffers nothing?

"Charity envieth not." Let him who can, deem it a slight perfection to be free from every taint of that wretched and selfish sentiment; let him who can, rejoice that he neither envies the superiority, nor is jealous of the advancement of friend or rival; that he can look on without regret, and see them outstrip him in the race; can exult in their praises, admire their excellencies, and conceal their faults, as much as his own; and act gladly upon the rule, "in honor preferring one another." Let him rejoice; for he has cause; if, glowing with the love of all that merits praise, and appreciating well the advantages of prosperity, the worth of reputation, and the inestimable happiness of being beloved, he is never stung by that scorpion of jealousy, which many may hate and scorn and conquer, and still feel and fear. Too often, if the heart speak in the words, there is small resistance to so odious an enemy. Else, why that evident pleasure in allusions to all that can degrade the rich, the able, the eminent; that habit of carefully intimating that the wealthy can be beneficent without feeling the cost; that the beautiful know their beauty, or have little beside it;

that one rose from an humble origin; that another has secret mortifications and trials; that another, though meritorious, is yet esteemed somewhat beyond his merit? Whence that anxiety, lest some warm heart should possibly cling to a friend, without seeing a fault? Be not deceived: the tones of envy are heard on every side; not always uttered with personal hostility, but breathing the wish that *none* may be lifted, whether by natural endowments, or by providential events, or even by eminence in goodness, too far above our level.

"Charity vaunteth not itself." The same spirit which envieth not, desires not to awaken envy. A vaunting temper is that which obtrudes in any manner a claim to superiority: that claim can be sustained only by the inferiority of others: charity desires not that inferiority. It aspires to advance, not necessarily to excel; for all may share in the advancement, but excellence implies that many are surpassed by a few. Alas, our innate corruption has bound together the ambition to do successfully all that we have to do, and the ambition to do it more successfully than other men; and it is the task of charity to separate them.

"Charity is not puffed up." Forbearing to vaunt itself, it does not recompense itself by cherishing within the pride which it would not disclose. As the feeling of hatred is as truly a sin against our neighbour as the act of revenge, so, exultation in the thought of superiority above him, is very nearly allied to the attempt to make him conscious of its existence. He who vaunts himself, displays to the world the extent of his ability: he who is puffed up congratulates himself that he is able, if he would, to display much more. The charitable man rejoices in what he possesses; but would rejoice also to make it the possession of all, in greater abundance than his own.

"Charity doth not behave itself unseemly." It studies all which is becoming, all which is courteous; and what is so graceful and so seemly as open and true kindness of heart? The time has not yet come, even in the bosom of Christian society, to forget this characteristic, or deem it supplied through the refinement of the age or the common forms of respect. Who has not seen, who that felt for the honor of the Gospel and the power of Christian example, has not deplored the sad spectacle of unseemly speech and conduct, even in religious publications, even in men who have thrown themselves into the front rank of the advocates of truth? Not by such aid shall truth be made to stand. Let us take heed, that in the utmost ardor of opinion or determination, the seemliness of moderation and modesty, of gentleness and benevolence, be never trodden down. Oh, never may we be successfully tempted, first to disguise religion by clothing it with the harshness and rudeness of our own minds, and then to drag Christian love, a bleeding victim, to its own altar!

"Charity seeketh not her own." Without a sigh it parts with much which it might justly claim, and will not hazard the violation of the bond of peace, for the sake of averting a slight sacrifice. If justice be done to our rights, our abilities, our motives, it is well: if not, it may easily be borne. To seek our own does not indeed import always a breach of amity: and it is only when this is risked, that even charity need forbear. For sacrifices of any personal interest, without an end in view, can of course be neither the part of wisdom, nor of duty, nor of kindness. But that spirit, wherever it may be found, which will have, at whatever cost to the feelings of other men, the uttermost farthing of its due, the whole credit of all which it has accomplished, every token of respect attached to its station, every evidence of gratitude deserved by its benefits; that spirit is not the character of a faithful disciple of Him who disarmed, for our sake, the law of perfect justice.

"Charity is not easily provoked." Mildness and meekness of temper are too much regarded as the gifts of nature, and not the triumphs of grace. Many men, from youth to age, are accustomed to yield without any show of earnest resistance, to the heat of an irritable mood; and seem to believe themselves fully excused by the temperament which has been given them. They are excused, indeed, for susceptibility, but not for being provoked to speak and act beneath its influence. If nature be at fault, it is a kind of deformity which must be counteracted by long and constant effort. Self-control is a feature that cannot be wholly wanting in the picture of a Christian.

"Charity thinketh no evil." It is esteemed in the world a most valuable trait of character, to discover with keen sagacity the selfishness and deceitfulness which may be hidden under some fair appearance. It is very reasonably believed that wisdom and experience impart such discernment. But wo, wo to him who, misled by a false construction of truths like these, accustoms himself to look earnestly and exclusively for some cause of suspicion; to conjecture where none can be proved, and to deny himself, by every artifice, the privilege of bestowing confidence, respect and love! The question itself may seem uncharitable; but it is constrained by appearances which, if they be not mistaken, would demand reproof from the lips of charity herself; are not some of us in the habit of deliberately supposing a worse motive for many actions of many persons, when these actions may be traced with even more plausibility to a better? Is not this the rule of judgment, applied by some of us to the conduct of all men, as if it betokened sound wisdom, to doubt the existence of sincerity or disinterestedness? Is it not with others the first, uniform thought, when the actions of some individuals are to be construed, who have become the victims of their prejudice? A Christian need not place himself in the hands of any; but if it be the habit of his mind thus to think evil, well may he turn his suspicions upon himself, and question whether he possess the grace, which is greatest of all.

"Charity rejoiceth not in iniquity, but rejoiceth in the truth;" and here again we ask, what is the cause of that strange pleasure, which, speaking in the look, the manner, the eagerness to spread the tale, declares itself too clearly to be mistaken, when iniquity has been done, and shame incurred, especially by a person of an opposite party or opinion? To rejoice in the guilt and disgrace of our own friends might indeed be too unnatural and horrible; but when we are arrayed in controversy which has enlisted all our feelings, are we not tempted to a dreadful satisfaction, if some disclosure confirm us, by testifying that our adversaries cared nothing for the truth?

"Charity beareth all things." With a calm gaze, fixed on the lasting, everlasting good of man, of every man, it can bear the little ills inflicted by human folly, ingratitude and perverseness. Much may be borne from those whom we truly love; much of infirmity, much of pain, much of wrong and cruelty. When was a mother weary of bearing with the very crimes of a child, so long as she could imagine his restoration possible with God? What if the world, then, insensible to its own highest interest, should repay the warm endeavors of the good with indifference, scorn, ridicule, insult? If they love their fellow-men, they surely can bear it, in hope of a better end: how much more those slight encroachments on their patience, their time, their benevolence, which are merely the results of forgetfulness and weakness!

"Charity believeth all things." While it maintains its own independence, and, knowing the prevalence of wickedness, and the infirmities of all men, will not expose important interests to any hazard which may be avoided; it yet presumes, till opposite proof be clear and multiplied, that what is asserted is true; that the avowed motive or intention is the real; that men are what they declare themselves.

There are assertions, however, which cannot be believed; and even charity must yield to evidence. It believeth all things which are capable of belief; and when their limit is reached, it still "hopeth all things." The adverse proofs are augmented; it hopes that they may yet be repelled. They become overwhelming; it hopes that the act may still be explained, without involving necessary guilt. The guilt is established; it hopes that it may yet be repented.

"Charity endureth all things." When hope is past, and that which is most dark is most certain, charity desires not to take into its hand the scourge of retaliation. "Vengeance is mine, I will repay, saith the Lord;" and if it might be, in consistency with the glory of God and the universal good, that even that recompense might be averted, charity would never cease to implore such clemency. Its spirit is expressed in that which was said of a Christian bishop,

> "Some write their wrongs in marble; he, more just,
> Stooped down serene, and wrote them in the dust:
> Trod under foot, the sport of every wind,
> Swept from the earth, and blotted from his mind,
> There, buried in the dust, he bade them lie,
> And grieved they could not 'scape th' Almighty's eye."

The limits of a single discourse have forbidden that more should be offered than the most rapid and general view of this heavenly character. But, general and rapid as it is, it is sufficient to place before you the aspect which that character has ever borne, where it has appeared amongst men. It cannot be denied that, so far as the eye can reach, it has been much more signally developed in some classes of Christian men than in others; nor that it has sometimes been hardly visible, where much of apparent zeal shone and blazed widely. But zeal, my brethren, may be engaged in any cause; charity is the spirit that comes down from heaven alone. If this be absent, it is not we, but the word and Spirit of God, that declare all zeal and faith and deeds to be worthless. In the day of judgment it may perhaps be seen, that many, who were regarded on earth as too lenient; as credulous and easily deceived; as persons merely amiable and kind, but not burning and shining lights; were indeed the brightest examples of that character which is most loved, approved and recompensed on high.

My brethren, if this mere review of the traits of charity, Christian charity have awakened in you no personal shame, no solemn awe, at the comparison of yourselves with the divine description, you have not shared the feelings of the preacher. I know of few Scriptures or none, more searching in their application to the thoughts of our hearts. If such be the image which we must bear, before we can be meet for the inheritance of the saints in light, how much is still to be wrought by the Holy Ghost upon our souls! What a broad gulf of separation still lies between the shores of peace and the selfish, the uncharitable world! No power except the mighty power of the grace of God can make us the living impressions of this picture. If none of its features be seen in us, oh, let us implore, as for our life, the gift of a new and contrite heart. If the resemblance be confused and dim, let us not faint nor be weary in the warfare with ourselves, till the greatest of all graces shall gird all the rest, like a resplendent zone, the bond of peace and of all virtues.

SERMON XV.

PERSONAL IMPROVEMENT.

Philippians, iv. 8.

"FINALLY, BRETHREN, WHATSOEVER THINGS ARE TRUE, WHATSOEVER THINGS ARE HONEST, WHATSOEVER THINGS ARE JUST, WHATSOEVER THINGS ARE PURE, WHATSOEVER THINGS ARE LOVELY, WHATSOEVER THINGS ARE OF GOOD REPORT; IF THERE BE ANY VIRTUE, AND IF THERE BE ANY PRAISE, THINK ON THESE THINGS."

PERSONAL improvement in all excellence is the theme of the text and of the present discourse. It is the career which is placed by the word of God before all the servants of our heavenly Master. "Be ye perfect," is his rule, "even as your Father which is in heaven is perfect;" a rule, not less appropriate to every other virtue than to that impartial kindness of which at first it was spoken. To employ every talent is the duty imposed by the very possession. To be all which our Maker endued us with powers to become, must be the law of our nature. To follow the footsteps of the Lord Jesus is our calling, as we are Christians; and there is no excellence, which was not a part of his perfect example. The divine commandments cannot fall below the highest worth to which each mortal, in his station, can aspire; and the grace of the Holy Spirit will not leave a single faithful effort without strong and sufficient support.

But, while we speak of personal improvement, let us take heed, at the beginning, that we assign it not an office which belongs to no labors of a sinner. If you are entreated to think on whatsoever things are true, or honest, or just, or pure, or lovely, or of good report, it is not that thus you may be prepared to claim, as the righteous reward of your diligence, a crown of celestial honor. It is not as if all could ever change the attitude in which we who have sinned and come short of the glory of God, must bow ourselves, when we seek a place in the kingdom of our Saviour. It is not as if there were in us the strength or skill to clothe ourselves with such moral excellence, so that, when we should have thought upon these things, we might exult in the character which had been formed as purely our own successful achievement. They who are thus exhorted by

St. Paul, are those who, with a true repentance, have turned to God, and by a lively faith, have put on Christ, and are now endeavoring to walk in the Spirit, as by the Spirit alone they live. The forgiveness of all our dreadful departure from this excellence, must be obtained through that ransom alone, which the love of God has provided for our souls; the precious blood of Christ, as of a Lamb without blemish, slain for the sins of the world. The power, warmly to love and truly to follow all things in which there is virtue or praise, the praise of God as well as of men, must be bestowed by the Holy Ghost. When all is ended, and we have won every excellence, in any measure, we shall still have done but our duty; we shall have left so much of that duty undone, that we shall be but unprofitable servants, without a claim on recompense or even on pardon, except as we are believers on Him through whom the ungodly are justified. But, when for his sake you hope for forgiveness and acceptance, and when in yourselves you feel the impulse of the Spirit to follow holiness, without which no man shall see the Lord, then every thought on the will of your reconciled Father and your Saviour, every wish to be found faithful to your trust, all your care for your preservation in the truth, all your desire to save the souls of your fellow-men, all your new-born delight in all goodness, will bid you think on these things.

There is no need to pause long at the words which form, in the text, such various names for high moral excellence. Things which are true, and honest or honorable, and just, and pure, and lovely, and of good report, may be indeed distinguished from one another, as may the colours in the bright bow which over-arches the skies. But all must blend themselves in one glorious light; and it is the evident design of the Apostle, not to urge their distinctions, but rather to embrace, through the accumulation of names, all which could ever be pursued for its moral worth or beauty. He enjoins us that we study all personal improvement, in every sphere in which our place is given us by Providence, in every feature of our character, at every successive stage of its development, till we shall see our Lord as he is, and be like him in perfectness. I would but attempt to suggest, in the most practical manner, some applications of a rule, which, lofty as it is, will avail but little, except it be brought into the constant, daily thoughts and duties where lies our conflict.

First, let it be remarked, that all these things are to be studied; that personal improvement in them all is to be a subject of earnest consideration. If I err not, there is here, in many Christian people, the most criminal carelessness. It seems scarcely to enter into their habitual view, that they are set in their several stations for this very purpose; and that all which befalls them, in the order of Providence, is designed to assist its accomplishment. They are thinking of their happiness, not of their improvement. Their wish is for salvation; but it offers itself to them, as deliverance from danger and wo, not from guilt and sin. You are surrounded, perhaps, by some distress or peril or confusion; your mind is burdened with anxiety; and you long for a condition of greater freedom, tranquillity and joy. But, in the mean time, there are, in your present state, some opportunities of virtue and of praise, which could be afforded by no other. Patience in suffering, magnanimity under injuries, inward calmness amidst outward confusion, cheerful confidence in the Lord, even when his face may seem to be hidden; these things are true, and just, and lovely. Are you solicitous to attain and to maintain them, till the hour shall be past; or do you sink under the trial, because you have not thus considered your lot? This is but one example: a thousand will appear to the eye which watches the springs of human conduct. It is thus that we so often notice the painful spectacle of a good man, a man acknowledged by all as a sincere and pious Christian, yet disfigured by faults, the most unamiable and repelling. He has not thought; he has not studied it as a high duty, to shake them off, one by one, if it might not be otherwise. He has fixed his determined stand: his part is taken, and so taken, that it admits no question: the general course of his life is in the path of uprightness; but he is not considering the effect of all his actions, nor the comprehensiveness of his rule of duty. A severer judge will often ascribe a severer blame; but it is enough for charity to say, that the absence of such consideration is itself a breach of the commandment. Think, then, of these things: let the thought of them become so much a habit, that all the changing events of life may point at once, each to the improvement which each was designed to forward. Think of the faults which are to be removed; think of the character to which you are called; compare the acts of each day with the standard that comprehends all things, "wherever there is any virtue, and wherever there is any praise." Thus, in a just consideration, you will establish the impulse to a steadfast advancement.

We observe, secondly, the extent of the apostolic precept. It reaches to *whatsoever* things are true, honest, just, pure, lovely and of good report. Nothing which bears such a character can be beneath attention or beyond the sphere of duty. It is easy to be content with great virtues, or virtues of imagined greatness; which perhaps have seldom an occasion for their exercise, or which may cost less of unceasing watchfulness. The desire is not unknown to many breasts, of balancing such virtues over against the smaller defects, which, it is hoped, will scarcely be noticed by mankind. Yet, if these defects be indeed little regarded, a triumph over them, through the power of religion, may, for that very reason, be more marked as the attestation of a conscientious spirit. To exhibit one or another of what are sometimes called the minor virtues, may be the effect of temperament, education, or some other accident; to exhibit them all, is almost the highest proof of moral effort, strong, persevering and victorious. Ask yourselves, therefore, and deem not the questions below the dignity of a Christian or the sanctity of the holiest hours; is there nothing which is worthy of study and esteem, in any of those lesser qualities, which we are accustomed to disregard? Is there nothing true in the faithful performance of all engagements, whatever may be the seeming measure of their importance; nothing in that degree of punctuality, which avoids so lavish a waste of the time of others; nothing in the endeavor not to mislead through slight exaggerations and perversions? Is there nothing honest, honorable, graceful, in the mantle of secrecy thrown silently over all within our knowledge, which our brother could rightly wish to be secret; or, on the other side, in the undisguised avowal of our own thoughts, intentions, and conduct? Is it not just, to prove, in the transactions of business, that we will never acquiesce in deceit, though it be sanctioned by wide custom; and, in political, yes, and in ecclesiastical contentions, that we will never seek an advantage for ourselves by abuse or misrepresentation or any of the sins against candor or kindness? Is there nothing pure in conversation always unstained by one word of indelicacy or of profanity needlessly repeated, to point a tale or a jest? Is there nothing lovely in the forbearance, which, striving to cast lightly aside the shafts that may wound our own feelings, strives also never to inflict the slightest of unnecessary pains on the feelings of another; nothing in the acquisition of that cheerfulness which carries pleasure wherever it passes; nothing in overcoming the thousand temptations to impatience, resentment, or vanity, from which none are exempt? Is there no good report, which justly joins itself to industry, to promptness, to accuracy, to decision, to constancy, to generosity? Oh, let us not deem the sphere of such exertions too humble, lest it should prove in the end far higher than our attainments! Nor let it be imagined that the rule of Christian worth extends not to pursuits which may seem to be but somewhat remotely connected with questions of morality. If it be right to do, it is right to do well. There is virtue and there is praise in some one course, whatever may be the employment of the hour: that course be it ours to follow. Let us be skilful in our occupations, so far as we have received the ability to attain such skill: let all that we attempt be accomplished, with an attention not indeed more than proportionate to its importance, but needful to its success. Religion hallows all; and the character which is thus formed in other employments, becomes also that which is maintained in the more peculiar walks of piety. He whose aim is every where else to be perfect, will not sink, as a Christian, into contented unworthiness. The details of our conduct, therefore, and of all our conduct, are subject to this broad injunction, "think on these things."

We remark, in the third place, that the precept of the text is the best safeguard for perpetual contentment and happiness. It gives us employment; employment without interruption; employment for ends, the highest, the most sacred, the most beneficent. It provides an antidote for every poison; a solace under every grief; a triumph in every trial. For we can be called to no scene, which is not for us a school of duty. Survey it as such; think that to this very spot the Lord, your Maker and Father, has now brought you; and inquire with what design? Surely, that now, upon this very spot, you might fulfil its appropriate duty, whatsoever it be, and thus enjoy the best happiness, if not always the brightest. Is it poverty that oppresses you? Study the cheerfulness that best adorns the poor; and when envy has been banished, and a patient trust in God has been settled, and a thankful heart rises in praise for those blessings which visit all, in truth you are richer than the wealthy. Is it a bereavement, which you mourn? Then it is the chastening hand of God; and while you feel that the peaceable fruits of righteousness are growing up in the midst of your sorrow, you are assured that the house of mourning is better than the house of feasting. Many and weary days and nights of bodily suffering are borne with tranquil peace, when the heart has once addressed itself faithfully to its task of cultivating a meek and patient endurance. The discontent, the frequent wretchedness, which is felt under these or under far lighter evils, is very much the effect of forgetting that affliction brings with it its own order of duties. We accustom ourselves to think of time which is not useful in assisting our worldly enjoyment, as therefore useless; we lament that we are excluded from so many means of doing and receiving good, and while we thus hold ourselves unemployed, we may well be weary of suffering. Then every vexing circumstance, however trivial, has power to disturb us; because each seems without a purpose. Thus, also, so many, in the fullest prosperity, are yet restless and dissatisfied; their hours are heavy and slow; and they are tempted to seek some miserable relief; only because they are not placing before themselves this noble labor of improvement. Think upon all those things in which there is any virtue, and in which there is any praise; on those especially which belong to your own condition and powers; and they will bring such occupation as brings also the worthiest of all pleasures.

To think upon these things, to fix our aim on all personal improvement, embraces, fourthly, the ready acknowledgment of faults, the acceptance of every reproof or suggestion, and the constant attempt to correct all blemishes, as well as to increase all actual excellencies. No doubt the mightiest hindrance, which checks the advancement of many, is the vain habit of lingering in thought, at that which they have already attained, instead of forgetting, like the apostle, those things which are behind, and reaching forth unto those things which are before. A thousand errors, too, are but faintly perceived by ourselves, while they are open to all others; and there is none to urge their amendment, only because a natural pride might repel the counsel. The friend forbears, through his reluctance to give pain, or his fears of cooling the warmth of friendship. The foe, perhaps, speaks, and speaks loudly; but how few are they who are wise enough to learn even from an enemy! It is, indeed, a weakness to surrender our own judgment to every advice; and he who should court counsels from every side, and consent to adopt each, would but be like a wave of the sea, driven with the wind and tossed. Still it is itself a token of high improvement, and it is the sure pledge of improvement yet more exalted, when the suggestion of a fault, from whatever source, and in whatever manner it may come, is made the immediate origin of an inquiry. It is nobler yet, when the result of such inquiry is the prompt and faithful endeavor to amend, if amendment was needed; and when is it not needed, if not always where the blame was attached, yet in some neighboring feature? Let us not pause very long to search for the motive of him who points us to the error. The kindest construction will be very often the truest; but his motive may not affect the merits of his charge or his recommendation. Our mortified pride may breathe suspicions; but let them be cast at once away. Pride is indeed the bitterest, subtlest foe of our improvement. It turns our eye afar from the field of labor; and bids us contend with the finder of the fault, not with the fault itself.

Let us be mindful of our true task; and suffer not the momentary sting of wounded vanity to delay our progress. If there be any virtue, and if there be any praise, there lies our Christian way; and virtuous it is, and worthy of all praise, to gather moral profit from every source; to become fools that we may be wise; and to begin our improvement with the acknowledgment of error. It is enough to assume the attitude of defence where we are constrained by some high principle, or when our very rectitude is injuriously assailed; but faults of judgment, of manners, of habit, of temper, of skill, are better owned without a struggle, that so they may be removed with the more alacrity. The mind that is intent on all improvement, if it do not invite reproaches, will not reject them, and will gladly draw from all men every just correction; from friends, with thankfulness; from adversaries, with that best revenge, which lies in the removal of the cause of accusation.

Finally, we must not leave the precept of the text, without notice of the place which it gives to the opinion of mankind. It certainly guides the Christian by a higher rule, when it commands him to think of all things which are true, and just, and pure, where there is any virtue. But when it unites with these, all those things, too, which are honorable, which are lovely, which are of good report, and where there is any praise, it seems also to cherish the desire for a worthy reputation and for the well-won love of our fellow-men. At least, it cannot be denied, that it enjoins upon us to seek all things which can purchase a blameless and a beloved name, and to seek them in this their character, as they are lovely and of good report. I know not why we should fear to encourage such a motive, when it is carefully held in subordination to the will of our God and Saviour. Nor will it, I apprehend, be found that those who are most susceptible to its influence are, for that cause, less watchfully obedient to the great law of divine love, or less studious of purity for its own honored sake. For, far from desiring the praise of men more than the praise of God, they desire it no longer and no farther than men are led to praise that which God has made to be praiseworthy. They ask not praise, indeed; but they would aim to be stainless, and would cherish no insensibility to the warm esteem of such as they cannot but esteem in return.

But, whatever be the motive, it is the command, that if there be any praise, we think on those things. No man is justified in feeling or in feigning indifference to the judgment of his brethren. As disciples of Christ Jesus, we are entrusted with the honor of his Gospel. We must not suffer it to be despised, through our deficiency. We must strive to commend it to all the world, by the cultivation of all things which reason prompts them to honor. Not on men as they may chance to be at the moment and just around us, must our thoughts repose: for where there is virtue, it often happens that there is no present praise, but rather digrace and persecution. But think of the judgment of men in their more thoughtful and better days; of the judgment of the time to come; of the judgment which they pronounce over the graves of the departed; and you will commonly observe that a good report on earth responds to the approving sentence of the Son of God.

SERMON XVI.

THE GOOD MAN.

Acts, xi. 24.

"For he was a good man."

This was spoken of the Apostle Barnabas. It is given as the cause of that joy with which his heart overflowed when he saw the Gospel of our Lord Jesus Christ, till then confined to men of Jewish birth, now taking deep and wide root amongst the Greeks at Antioch. He was sent down from Jerusalem to see and to guide that blessed work; and because "he was a good man, and full of the Holy Ghost, and of faith," he rejoiced to give it his best labors, and to bring a still stronger arm, that of Saul of Tarsus, to enter into those labors.

The Apostle Barnabas is but one of the good men of the Scriptures. However interesting were the time and the circumstances in which he thus appears, there are other histories of good men and their acts in the same divine record, which are as instructive and as eminent. Goodness, at different periods, may be differently occupied, while it remains the same throughout all time, in every variety of character, and even under every dispensation; the same image of God, in the soul of man, created by the Holy Ghost, through that faith without which it is impossible to please God. But if we would so study it that it may become our own, we must think of a goodness which shall be exercised not so much in scenes like those through which apostles, prophets and patriarchs went on to heaven, as rather here, in this day, when the world and the church are what they are. We must not be content or anxious to wear the robes, but only to have the spirit, of the saints of old.

Taking, then, these few and simple words which describe one good man under the new covenant, we ask, where and what manner of man is he, to whom emphatically this praise is given by the Spirit of God, and shall be given in the day when the righteous shall go into life eternal? May that blessed Spirit teach us to know and love and seek such goodness as comes from heaven, and prepares for heaven, through Jesus Christ our Lord!

A good man is not such by nature. No happy combination of bodily temperament and mental powers; no harmony of faculties; no sweetness of disposition; no inborn love of peace; no gentleness or kindness, like that which sometimes beams from the eye and speaks in the tones of the voice, and yet is found capable of uniting itself with much indulgence in guilt; no natural character of the natural man, however attractive it may be, can form the great distinction between them that do good and them that do evil.

A good man is one who owns and feels that in himself, in his own carnal nature, there dwelleth no good thing, but that what he is, so far as he is good, he is by the grace of God, which has renewed his nature, and made him a new man in Christ Jesus. He is one who has been convinced by a thousand and ten thousand words, acts and thoughts of his own, by the experience of all his days and his years, that, left to himself, he would be at the best but a reed shaken with the wind, and might be borne on from sin to sin, from temptation to temptation, towards any gulf of guilt and horror. Thus convinced of sin, he has fled, and he still flees, for pardon and for hope, to the Lamb of God, who taketh away the sins of the world; to the mercy-seat, sprinkled as it is with the blood of the atonement. There he has asked and received, both forgiveness and renewal; the grace that justifies through the merits of his Redeemer, and the grace that sanctifies by the power of the Holy Ghost. He has died to sin, and he has risen to newness of life. All his goodness has begun with the prayer for mercy, and with the mercy which has answered to his prayer.

From the time when he first called upon God with an earnest and believing heart, he has inquired what the Lord would have him to do; and when he knew the will of God, to do it indeed has been his humble, honest endeavor. The knowledge of his own sinfulness, the love of God in Christ, the blessed hope of a heavenly inheritance which he could never deserve, all are but mightier motives to glad and grateful obedience for the time to come. He has entered on a course which embraces all the duties of doing justly, loving mercy, and walking humbly with his God; it is to be his aim to fulfil all righteousness. From the rule, imperfect as his fulfilment must ever be, from the rule itself he neither asks nor desires exemption.

Such an one, like Barnabas, like Saul, like

every Christian in their days, has not delayed to confess Christ in his ordinances and in the fellowship of his people. He has not hesitated to assume, before all men, the baptismal covenant. He has drawn near with faith to the table of the Lord, and taken that holy sacrament to his comfort. He is every where recognized as a member of the Church of Christ, in constant communion with his brethren, through the breaking of bread, through prayer, and through all the acts and offices in which, as a member, he can contribute to the health and growth of the whole body. Like Barnabas, he rejoices when a door is opened any where for the entrance of the Gospel, but especially when the tidings come that the heathen who knew not God, are flying to the sound as doves to their windows. Like Barnabas, he is prepared to render in such a cause, that service to which, whatever it be, he is called by his own place and powers. "A good man, full of the Holy Ghost, and of faith," is a strong pillar in the support of all goodness, and righteousness, and truth, in an evil world.

He of whom the text was written, was an eminent minister of Christ; the second great apostle to the Gentiles. The minister of Christ, whatever be his degree or station, should be, before all things, "a good man;" and if he be not, his portion can be only that of Balaam, to bless the tents of Israel, to wish for the death of the righteous, but to die in his own iniquity; or that of Iscariot, to betray the cause which he has been called and has promised to serve, and then to close all with despair. But a good man, engaged as a messenger of the Lord, and commending himself to every man's conscience, is one who both

"Allures to brighter worlds, and leads the way."

His life sustains the doctrine which he proclaims: he is himself a living epistle, speaking the truth in love, as the Spirit of God has written it upon his heart, to be known and read of all men.

But Christian ministers, numerous as they should be, yet should be and are but a small proportion of the good men who have been formed by the Gospel. "Let every man abide in the same calling wherein he is called," says the Apostle Paul; making this the general rule, while the special summons to ministerial labor is the exception, though certainly the frequent exception. In every calling, in every station, there is abundant room and occasion to glorify God and adorn the doctrine of Christ by walking as He walked, in innocence, holiness and usefulness. The private path was that which he trod through much the greater portion of his earthly sojourn. The exhortations of the apostles always contemplate the body of Christians as occupied in the common business and sustaining the usual relations of society, while the love of God, the patient waiting for Christ, and the constant preference of the things which are eternal, separate them from the world, and mark them as a peculiar people. Good men will be known as such, even in the busiest scenes of labor, commerce or counsel, by their uprightness, their sincerity, their diligence in the discharge of every task, and their conscientious acknowledgment of a law above all social laws, which binds them in all things to do as they would that others should do to them, and as He did whose meat and drink it was to do the will of his Father. They need no apology for conduct which the world itself has pronounced selfish or treacherous; no explanation of transactions of doubtful integrity; no difficult pleas of the charity that covereth a multitude of sins, and hopeth all things. Oh, there are Christians for whom, living and dying, their brethren hope, while yet the thought of them as "good men" does not spring up involuntarily in the mind, as if that were their plain and chief characteristic, spreading its light and its fragrance through all the rest. But so should it be with all those who name the Lord Jesus Christ as their Redeemer, and confess that he has purchased them, to be his servants.

There are other scenes in which good men alone are active. They alone go about doing good. They alone exercise that true devotion, which consists both in keeping themselves unspotted from the world, and in visiting the fatherless and widows in their affliction. They alone so love the souls of their fellow-men, as to enter with glowing hearts into every effort to bear to them, and spread amongst them, and urge upon them, the message of salvation. To them alone are the interests of the spiritual body of Christ so dear and precious, that their right hand shall sooner forget its cunning than they forget Jerusalem. Others may be open to many an impulse of humanity and compassion. Others, from indifference, from importunity, or from a naked and cold sense of duty, may cast into the treasury which aids in sustaining the work of missions. Others may appreciate the order, the historical recollections, and the many social blessings of the Church, and feel a certain zeal for its prosperity, especially within their own near borders. So much is possible without that goodness which is the fruit of the Spirit. But in the Christian alone, in the truly good man only, is benevolence a spiritual thing, and uniform, and universal. He knows no more engaging business and no richer delight. He turns not from this occupation to others for his refreshment, but from others to this.

The talents with which good men have been entrusted, are very various. Whatever they may be, they are employed, freely employed, for the same bounteous and gracious ends for which the Lord of heaven and earth scatters every where his mercies. All are held in stewardship: all are his, and are acknowledged to be subject to his command and to his declared designs. As he is good, and his mercies are over all his works, so it is his will that his servants, the good men of each generation, should, each in his place, be the benefactors of their brethren; and such they are. If they have high gifts of intellect, the first and best offerings of their powers are consecrated to the honor of the great Giver, and to the guidance, instruction and happiness of men. If they have wealth, they have no wish to heap it higher and higher as a throne for their own exaltation; but gladly dispense it far and wide, till the blessings of many are upon them, and they have laid up on high a good foundation against the time to come. So, the good man of the text, Barnabas, the Levite of Cyprus, "having land, sold it, and brought the money, and laid it at the Apostles' feet," while he offered himself also to the service of Christ and his Gospel. If good men have but their own personal activity, energy or industry, their own faithful example, and voice, and co-operation with others, whom they must follow rather than lead, yet these they gladly offer. They seek not high things; refuse not even their little because it is little; but take the post which has been assigned them, and only strive that the work of heavenly love may be done; by their own hand, if no other is prepared, but by any hand, if it be but done effectually. The good man is known by his readiness for every good word and work, whatever be the talents which fit him for one post or another. Every where there is room; room for the humble, the patient, the industrious, the persevering, to serve God and do good, with ten talents or with one, and in the self-same spirit.

These things may be seen; but if you ask

for the source of these things, you must trace them to a point, beyond which no human eye can enter. There is a life within, which gives to the outward life of the good man its heavenly form and expression. He is one who prays without ceasing; one to whom the word of God is sweeter than the honeycomb, and therefore is his habitual study and meditation; one whose waking purposes at the dawn, whose noonday aspirations, whose evening self-examination, and whose thoughts in the silent midnight watches, alike ascend to the Fountain of all goodness, through the mediation of the Son of Man, who is the Son of God. Therefore he comes forth with something in his appearance which is not wholly of this world; something which, however faintly, reminds you of the Master whom he serves, and of those who walked with God in the ancient days. A truly good man may have the manners of the society around him; may be quite unrecognized by the multitude as they hasten to and fro. Yet, be with him but a little while; let but that which is deepest in his soul be called to utter itself; and you shall see that he has there a temple and an altar, from which the incense of prayer and praise is continually ascending. He is indeed a temple of the Holy

Ghost, from whom all good works do proceed: they all begin with holy desires, and these are a part of that inward life, which can be fully known only to Him to whom the heart is open. But this is certain, that whosoever he may be amongst you, who is attracted by the loveliness of true goodness, to wish that it may be copied in his own life, must walk as seeing things that are invisible, must live in communion with God and in anticipation of heaven, if he would live outwardly as good men live, and do what they do for his brethren of mankind.

The path of the good man "is as the shining light, which shineth more and more unto the perfect day." It is a progress from strength to strength, from hope to hope still more confirmed and triumphant. The same causes which produce in him any thirst after righteousness, make him long for fresh draughts from that celestial fountain; and one who has truly wished to be good, must of necessity desire to be better and better, as he knows himself more, and sees more of his own sinfulness, and more of the love of God and the beauty of holiness. If there be Christians who seem to stand still, and Christians who seem to lose the ground which once they held, yet he in whom all acknowledge the "good man" of the Scriptures is one who is ripening towards the perfection which he still must always feel to be so distant. His heart is fixed: he loves goodness as the image of God, and delights in its excellence. Therefore he seeks it, and strives to grow in grace, and to add to his faith, virtue and every thing wherein there is praise, both that he may make his calling and election sure, and that he may be more and more truly the child of his heavenly Father, and the follower of his Saviour. Such an one must advance; and though, very often, as years diminish the physical energy, and as a calmer wisdom succeeds to youthful ardour, and as the Christian may be withdrawn into more private scenes, the world may the less take note of his progress, or even lose him from its sight, yet he is really drawing nearer to the angels, and partaking more and more of the spirit of those blessed beings whose only will is the will of God.

Let us follow the good man to the close. It comes in God's own time and manner. He cannot repine that he is called away from the service which he rejoiced to perform in the midst of much conflict and many temptations, and of a multitude that do evil, to such service as may be prepared for him where there is perfect peace, and freedom from all temptation, and no society but that of the pure and just. We speak not of him as without anxiety for his own safety. Many good men, deeply moved by their knowledge of the divine glory, and of their own unworthiness and manifold transgressions, their sins, negligences and ignorances, have contemplated eternity with a solemnity which was often painful and trembling. Yet, seldom indeed, I believe, does the good man who has been described, pass down into the vale of death without the light of the countenance of his Father, or without the rod and staff of the good Shepherd, to be his comfort. The angels of God have had charge over him to keep him in all his way; they minister to him as they are commanded; and they wait to receive him, like that righteous beggar who passed into Abraham's bosom. His goodness, the fruit of the Spirit, is the divine seal upon his spirit, marking him as an heir of glory. He has fought a good fight; and in him the evil one has no part; nor can he have his abode except with those who, like him, love God and goodness. "He that dwelleth in love, dwelleth in God, and God in him." "He that doeth good, is of God;" and as surely as the streams glide to the ocean, so surely does all true goodness tend towards its origin, and find its final home in heaven.

To be great, my dear brethren, to be wealthy, to be highly honored for talents, or station, or influence, or services of wide renown, is given to few, and is made the duty of none. To be good, is, through grace, within the power of all; and is required of all. However private, however humble the person, he can turn to God, love the Lord Jesus Christ, keep his commandments and walk in the way of life everlasting. The shadows of this earth are passing by; and we shall soon stand in the light of eternity and of truth. Then the only greatness, worth or excellence which can be acknowledged or valued, will be this; and the last on earth shall often be first in heaven, and the first last. The question whether we are desiring and seeking this character and portion for ourselves, is the great question which even now, in the sight of God, divides us into two great and opposite companies, whose paths are ever becoming more and more widely separate.

Those of you who have contemplated this character, and have seen in it nothing which you truly seek, are simply living without God, and repulsing all invitations to join the blessed company of just men made perfect. You must turn from the error of your ways, and embrace a better hope, or you must reap as you have sown. "They that have done good shall come forth to the resurrection of life; and they that have done evil, to the resurrection of damnation." It is the word of God: it is the law under which you are living, in expectation of immortality. You are going down to the grave without the character of good men, in the sense of the Scriptures. No other character will avail beyond the grave. Oh, that your prayer may be, "create in me a new heart, O God, and renew in me a right spirit!"

Such of you as are good men indeed, in that sense which the Spirit of God inspired and approves, may be slow to accept the title; and your humility is indeed your crown. Disturb it not; you have no merit; your religion ends as it began with the confession of unworthiness and sin; and your righteousness is but the gift of Him who alone in himself was righteous. Be humble, but persevere. The day is coming when every man shall have praise of God; and then may our place be with his, whose name is written in the book of revelation and in the book of life, as that of "a good man, full of faith and of the Holy Ghost!"

SERMON XVII.

FAMILY PRAYER.

Joshua, xxiv. 15.

"As for me and my house, we will serve the Lord."

Joshua, the faithful general of the Israelites, gave them their solemn choice between the service of the living God, and the service of idols. As for himself, his part was taken; and taken, not for himself only, but also for his household. It is on this that I would now fix your eyes; for, I propose to speak of a great office and duty of the heads of families. May God enable me rightly to speak, and you so to hear, that his blessing may be more abundantly on your homes and your children!

No man can give assurance that his house will continue to serve the Lord with spiritual, heartfelt piety, when he is gone, or even while he lives. The heart is beyond parental control; and Joshua never meant to promise that he would or could secure the lasting faithfulness of his race to the covenant of their God. He spoke as one, doubtless, who knew that their present sentiment was with his own; as one who had not unsuccessfully taught and trained them by counsel and example. He spoke also as their representative; as every man is authorized to declare the bounden duty of those who depend on him by natural obligation; and over whom he has received from God, the right of command. But he spoke moreover, as one who in certain things, in the outward services of the law, had the power as well as the right and the duty, to rule his own house, and to exact and enforce obedience, and who was resolved to exercise it for the honor of his Master.

Religion has its inward and its outward duties; God demands both alike. It is in vain to regard the feelings of the heart as if they were all; or as if they could exist either without outward means of care and nourishment, or without producing outward signs and actions. A father, you say, cannot make his children religious. It is true; but he can surround them from the first with all those customs and means which are appointed to assist them in choosing for themselves the service of God; he can instruct them in all the truths and duties of religion; he can prevent the formation of habits of wickedness; and he can insist that they shall, in their external conduct, display respect and reverence for the Lord, for his word, his day, and all his ordinances. By the law of God, given by Moses, the parent was bound to teach his son the meaning of the sacred festivals, and the contents of the law itself; to speak of the divine statutes frequently at home; when he lay down, and when he rose up; when he sat in the house, and when he walked by the way; and thus to be as it were the minister and teacher of his own household. He was also himself to offer for himself and his household, the paschal lamb, of which they all were to partake together; and together they sat down to eat of other sacrifices. Before the selection of Aaron and his descendants to be the priests of Israël, every man seems to have been for every purpose, the priest of his own family; and much of that character remained, and remains to this day. Some family worship was therefore a custom from the beginning. The very course of nature enjoins it, wherever religion itself has an existence. It seems impossible that a father who fears God, and feels the dependence of himself and his household upon the divine blessing, should forbear to express this in some manner by his conduct; and the natural expression is that of calling them together to unite with his, their praises and their prayers. Thus has arisen the custom of family prayer; and although there is no express command in Scripture, providing that it should take place every morning and every evening, yet we may boldly say that no such command was needful. Wherever a sense of religion should prevail, such a custom, once begun, would be widely followed. There is no express command that we should pray even in private, every morning, and every evening; yet, how can we conceive of piety, without some such exercises! The word of God commands us to pray always, without ceasing; this, at the least, must be daily and more than daily prayer; nature suggests the commencement and close of the day as the chief and most obvious seasons; and every impulse of time and order, of natural affection, and of parental duty, bids us, if we are at the head of families, gather around us at those seasons, our domestic circle.

I would exhort you, plainly and affectionately, to the practice of family devotion. The pastor cannot know, with some exceptions, in what families it is already a practice. It is not like many other duties, the observance or neglect of which is apparent to every acquaintance. The pastor cannot follow his people to their closets, nor even push his inquiries so far as to learn the private customs of every home. It may be well, perhaps, that I should not know whom I may censure, nor with few exceptions, who are securing to themselves the blessing which assuredly hovers over a household, where prayer is wont to be made.

This blessing is the first great consideration which shall persuade you to commence and continue the custom in your own houses. God is a hearer of prayer, and has often taught that the benefits and the evils which are the consequences of obedience or of guilt, do, in various ways, overflow from the individual upon those with whom he is connected, and especially upon his children. Every thing around us attests that this is a part of the providential government of society; and few stronger motives could be addressed in the heart, than the affection which constrains us to seek for our families all which we desire for ourselves, and even to wish to avert from them evils which for ourselves we are willing to hazard. The Lord has addressed this motive; and Scripture and observation assure us that his blessing, for them that love him, is upon children's children. Can any parent, who has the heart of a parent, be indifferent to the happiness, here and hereafter, of those who look to him for guidance, protection and example, and to whom he has even given life with all its uncertainties? Can any parent who believes that God "is, and that he is a rewarder of them that diligently seek him," doubt the power of the united prayers of a family to bring down upon itself that blessing which maketh rich for time and for eternity? When they are in danger, you feel that all is in the hands of God, and you do not question the efficacy of prayer to obtain deliverance. Surely it is as powerful, and it is as needful, when we do not perceive ourselves to be in immediate peril. Are we not every day dependent on the protection of Almighty God, and exposed to the sickness that walketh in darkness, and the destruction that wasteth at noonday? Dare we, without reference to divine help, consign a family even to the silent repose of a single night? But, oh, how much more than perils of sickness or accident, of plunder or of flame, is to be dreaded for that circle, if it be not under the wings of Almighty goodness! Do you think to bring up a family, and make it prosperous, and keep it in virtue, temperance, honesty, industry and harmony, without the blessing of him "from whom all holy desires, all good counsels and all just works proceed?" Dare you hold the responsibility which is upon you, without aid from heaven? Can you expect that aid unless it be sought? How shall it be sought, if not by that prayer which goes up from the bosom of the united family? Look on the one picture and then upon the other. See one family, rising only to eat and to drink, and to rush forth into all their worldly business, without a passing thought of God, so far as appears to the ear or eye; no lesson from his word, no thanks for the preservation of the night; enjoying their repast, and going out to their toils; and then returning at evening without notice of their Protector and Sovereign, whose laws they have broken, without petitions for forgiveness, without invocation of mercy, to lay themselves down and sleep, with as little reflection on any thing above themselves as the beasts that perish. See another family, gathered before a step is taken in the business of the day, to lift up their united voices in the words which Christ has taught, asking their daily bread, forgiveness of their trespasses, preservation from temptation and from all evil; hearing or perhaps reading together that word which shall be a light to their feet; giving thanks for the peaceful slumbers of the night; and then separating, to return at the evening, and to close all with another offering of thanks for the blessings of the day, and with united prayers for that pardon which each is sure to need, and that protection without which the watchman waketh but in vain. On which of these two families shall blessings descend from that God who heareth prayer? Which of these families is yours?

But even if the direct blessing to be sought and obtained were left out of sight, family prayer might well be recommended as one of the best means of promoting the good education, the order and the union of a family; and as such, would be worthy of adoption. There is no instruction or training like that which begins with the fear and the word of the Lord. From family prayers each child will proceed to all the labors and duties of the day with a sense of their importance and seriousness which nothing else can impart. Without family prayer, there is no thorough, inward principle of order and government there; no distinct reference to that which makes parental authority holy; the commandment of God, the delegation of his right and power to fathers and mothers. When you cast out religion from the habits of your houses, what do you leave behind for your support? Force and fear; such fear as you can inspire, such force as you can exercise. Oh, how much shorter and truer and more pleasing a course, to pray with them, and to teach them that, in obeying you, they obey their Maker and yours! If you would unite them with yourselves in love and duty, what method so sure as daily to unite your prayers at the footstool of a Father in heaven! Many parents who have themselves felt but too little the obligation of their duty and their debt to God, have yet appreciated enough the weight of these considerations, to preserve for their children's sake, the practice of family devotion. I would not thus press it upon you; but first as a duty to your common Maker, and a debt to the Author of all your blessings and your hopes; and then, and in a secondary respect only, as in itself a blessed means of establishing in your households good education, order and harmony. Prayer is never to be viewed as performed, in the first place, for any other purpose than its own sacred one; to ask and to receive. But it may not be improper to place the more indirect benefits of family prayer in a striking light, by supposing, for a moment, that just the same petitions would be separately offered, and the same portions of Scripture read, by each member of the family, in addition to their own private exercises of devotion. It may then be said that the several private petitions would as surely be answered as if they were all united at one spot. Yet who would not own in a moment that it was better that those who thus prayed apart for family blessings, should also come and pray for them together? Why? Because it would be so much more beautiful and appropriate, and adapted to unite all hearts in love, and to lend incitement and wings to the prayer of each by the impulse from the others, and to make a church of every Christian family, a church with its common worship. The Lord also has given a special encouragement to such union of prayer, by his special promise, where two or three are met in his name, and have agreed concerning the subject of their petitions. While he ordained and sanctified private prayer, he gave also his benediction to the union of hearts and voices, because it was good and comely.

Of the excellence of family prayer, however, every one, no doubt, is satisfied, who really feels the preciousness of the privilege of praying in any manner and at any season. That it is a duty, all such would probably feel, did they not imagine that the difficulties are often, and are in their own case, sufficient to justify neglect. Let us advert to some of the chief of these difficulties, with a real desire to know and enter the way of duty and of blessing, and not to be checked by trifles or by dreams.

It is thus objected, that it is sometimes impossible to collect a family with regularity in the morning or at evening. Doubtless, individuals must be sometimes so occupied, that their attendance is not to be expected. But in almost every family the members in general do assemble for their meals at the commencement and the close of the day; and if there be no other and better time, they can certainly hold then their family worship. So easily is this objection answered and removed.

It is a more serious objection, and really forms very often the true cause of the neglect, that there may be members of the family who would dislike the practice. But if those members are children or dependents, I would ask whether the duty of a parent or master is ever to be weighed in such balances. There are few children, perhaps, who would not, at one time or another, have wished to have been excused from their most important duties. There are as few who do not have cause to thank the care of parents, if their wishes have been disregarded, when these opposed their best advantage. Be assured that this plea of leaving it to the untaught, thoughtless choice of children, whether they shall or shall not be trained up in the ways of religion, will never be received at the bar of God. Parents are given to children for the very end that, during their early youth, they may answer for them, and choose for them, and guide and rule them with a wisdom which is not as yet their own. This question of family prayers should be decided by the conscience of the parent, not by the fancy of the children; and yet the apprehension that it would be a weariness to a well-trained family of children, is but a dream, suggested by indolence or timidity. Call them together; give each a Bible, and let them read alternately; and after they have attended family worship for a time, you will probably find that they would much regret to see it relinquished, and that, to their latest days, it will be one of the most precious of their domestic recollections. But it may be that those whose reluctance is feared, are older inmates of the family; and in that event all which can be said is, that such are to decide for themselves whether they will attend; but every family has its head, and the head is responsible for its government and regulations. I have been speaking to the heads of families; for with them this duty must rest. If they are unwilling, no other member can establish a family service; though sometimes, at their request, another may discharge the office. It should be the province of the father; and in his absence or inability, of the mother or of any other who may be old enough to undertake the office. There are few sadder signs in our days, than that in so many families, while other members would rejoice in the establishment of such services, the head should be most unready.

It will be objected by some that they are not able to express themselves in prayer; and this would indeed be a real and wide-spread difficulty, if family prayer must be extemporaneous. For, certainly, most persons, unaccustomed to public speaking or to framing addresses of any kind, would be and are incompetent to the task of preparing and uttering the devotions of others as well as their own at any moment. But there is no doubt, in my judgment, that, in general, a form of prayer is far better for family devotion, even with those who could dispense with its aid; and for those who cannot, it at once removes all the force of this objection. There are many excellent books of this kind; and any who may desire it, can, almost without cost, supply themselves, at least with a tract, containing family prayers for every morning and evening of the week. You have also in the Prayer Book one form, remarkably comprehensive, scripturally pure, always suitable; and surely, with these aids, no man who can read has any longer the excuse of inability.

The last and utmost objection, however, will be, that you shrink from an act so solemn. You are not, perhaps you say, professors of religion. If you were, your profession would certainly be one additional ground of earnest appeal; and should there be communicants at the head of families, who have no such practice, to them such an appeal is now most affectionately addressed. But surely the fact that you are not such, cannot excuse from this duty or from any other. The reply could come with force from no one except one who never prays at all; and from such an one family prayer is not to be demanded, while he thus remains in his sins, not knowing what shall be on the morrow. Him we can only exhort to repent, while yet it is called to-day; for there is but a step between him and everlasting condemnation. But why any person, who prays any where, should shrink from praying at the head of his own family, the place where God has appointed that he should stand, it is impossible to assign a reason, or the appearance of a reason, beyond that deplorable fear and shame, which so powerfully holds back many a man from his acknowledged duties, and from the way of life eternal.

My dear friends, let me beseech you to adopt, each of you, the resolution of Joshua, "As for me and my house, we will serve the Lord." Gather your family around you: open the Bible, and read, or let them read with you; and then kneel down with your Prayer Book, or your book of family devotions, and, commencing or closing with the Lord's Prayer, ask, and ye shall receive, for them and for yourselves. The tremulousness with which you begin, will be past in a week. You will be the stronger for every duty by having once overcome that weakness, and avowed before your own household that you wish to lead them and go with them to heaven. Having once begun, never relinquish this blessed custom; or if possibly you have already both begun and relinquished it, restore it without delay, and abandon it not again, if you would not sacrifice the blessing of an united and religious family. I add no more. Whether any heads of families will be moved thus to serve the Lord with their houses, they must determine, and the great day will declare. But he who would say in that day, "Behold, I and the children which God hath given me;" he who would make the home of his family the place of their education for usefulness, prosperity, love, obedience and heaven, let him, without delay, set up his family altar, and offer there a morning and an evening sacrifice.

SERMON XVIII.

THE TIME FOR SERVING GOD.

Ecclesiastes, xii. 1.

"Remember now thy Creator in the days of thy youth, while the evil days come not, nor the years draw nigh, when thou shalt say, I have no pleasure in them."

The text is most commonly introduced as an exhortation to the very young; and then it has all its force to the utmost. But as the evil days of which it speaks, and which are so strikingly described in the rest of the chapter, are plainly those of extreme old age and the approaching end, it is plain that the text may be addressed with great significance to *any* who have still a considerable time, if life be spared them, between themselves and that season of decay. If we strike out the words, "in the days of thy youth," the advice is one which all who have passed these days, but have not yet arrived at the opposite extreme, must feel to be not less necessary for them than for the youngest; nay, to be even more pressing. May God give to all alike a most deep and solemn conviction of what these words were intended to convey!

I would speak, from them, against the disposition, alas, so common, to postpone religion till the evil days indeed draw nigh. Not that old age is distinctly placed before the mind as the only or the fittest time for serving God; but that there is an impression as if life could be better enjoyed, while it has enjoyments, without the sanctifying power of religion, and as if, nevertheless, to let it close without that sanctifying power of religion were a most miserable end.

Let me place before you a few pictures. A youth, in all the bloom of his days, with health to spare, with every prospect of worldly advancement, beloved of friends, caressed by numerous acquaintances, and able to command the foremost place amongst the lovers of pleasure, approaches the communion-table; takes his stand as a Christian before the world; and endeavors to be useful in the Church of Christ, and to live soberly, righteously and godly. All around, you too often hear the language of something like astonishment, even where it is the language of approval. That such a path should have been chosen now, this it is which is seen as if it were a marvelous determination. Many a heart exclaims, on witnessing the spectacle, that he must be either a hero or an enthusiast; either capable of a very great height of virtue, or else liable to be charged with rashness and folly. Even prudent and pious people look on, and express their hopes that he will persevere, in tones which rather declare their fears that he will fall away.

A man of business, in all his vigor and success, finds time to think of the commandments of his Maker. He even denies himself some worldly advantages, and restricts himself for the sake of profit to his soul, from some opportunities of increasing his business and his gains. Perhaps, already rich enough, he resolves to be no richer, or at least to make no efforts to be rich, but to devote his future acquisitions chiefly to beneficence. Like Zaccheus, he exclaims, "Behold, Lord, the half of my goods I give to the poor." He declares that he means, by the grace of God, to do whatever he does, to the glory of God; and he devotes his best days, his best powers and his best efforts, to the service and promotion of the kingdom of heaven. The world, as before, sees it with astonishment.

Has any great trouble befallen him? Has he lost his property? Has he been bereaved of wife or children? Is his mind quite sound, and calm, and steady? The world treats it as a matter of some surprise, that a man, in the possession of perfect judgment, and capable of enjoying honor, and health, and wealth, should choose the way of God, and prefer an inheritance in heaven before them all.

But now turn to another picture. Yonder is an aged man, full of infirmities. His days upon earth are evidently numbered. His strength is but labor and sorrow. He is seen to be often engaged in solitary prayer. He turns over the leaves of his Bible with ever new satisfaction. He takes great pleasure in speaking of his hope in Christ, and his future abode with the saints above, and in offering to the young his word of advice that they remember now their Creator. When he is about to die, he assembles his children around him, gives them his blessing, and assures them, from all his experience, that the Lord is gracious to them that fear him, and put their trust in his mercy. All who behold such a scene, behold it with reverence. It is as they would wish their own venerable parents or friends to depart. "Let my last end be like his," is their general exclamation; and if, instead of all this, they saw an old man go down to the grave with blasphemies upon his lips, or even with the evident spirit of avarice and worldliness in his heart, all would recoil with a natural repugnance and horror.

Or, again, in the midst of his days, or even in early youth, some one is smitten with fatal disease. Perhaps he knows it; perhaps he knows it not; but it is perceived by others; and, with sinking hearts, they watch the fatal progress. How soon do they inquire, whether he is aware of his own condition; and how anxiously do they imagine what are his probable feelings, in anticipation of the close! How solicitous are his friends that he should labor under no delusion! How gladly do they perceive in him any signs of thoughtful concern, of faith, of hope, and of a conscience at peace through the blood of Jesus! Even the most indifferent are more than willing to hear that he has apparently found rest unto his soul; and all who are not utterly hardened, would, with pain, behold him walking on the verge of the grave, as unconcerned as the thousands who, in health and prosperity, are pursuing the several objects of their earthly desires. No one is surprised when such a person inquires with all the earnestness of an immortal being whose whole future happiness is at hazard, what he must do to be saved.

The difference between these two classes of pictures is simply this; that in the one sorrow and death are at hand, in the other at a distance. In the mode in which, in both classes, religious seriousness is regarded by the world, we perceive an evident opposition to the express words of Scripture. "Remember thy Creator," is his command, "while the evil days come *not*, nor the years draw nigh, when thou shalt say, I have no pleasure in them." But the world seems to say, "Remember thy Creator when those days and those years arrive, but wait till then: why shouldest thou suffer before the time?" And although, as men advance in years, they become quite accustomed to that by which at first they would have been smitten with dismay, yet I suppose that early in life, scarce one in a multitude could bear the thought of dying without hope in Christ, while nevertheless to live without such a hope, if all fear of death could be removed, would cause them no disturbance.

One occasion of these feelings is manifest. The great business of religion must be performed "while yet the lamp holds out to burn." If it has been neglected till the light is flickering and becoming extinguished, we must seize the hours which remain. Like every other labor which has been postponed till the allotted time is almost over, it will now demand the greater promptness and energy. It cannot be postponed any longer: it must be done now, if at all; now or never. The penitent himself seems striving to redeem, if it were possible, the consequences of his former delay, and can scarcely give a moment of attention, perhaps, to any thing except the one thing which is needful. His pious friends, conscious that the time is short, will act upon the plain and universal principle of placing first that which is most pressing, and will bestow upon him their cares and efforts, rather than on those who may have longer time and more numerous opportunities. A pastor may be expected to visit, admonish and instruct the sick much more frequently than such as are in health. More prayers are offered for the condemned criminal than for those who are more innocent, and far more able to do service to the cause of truth and righteousness. But where we perceive great efforts, there we are led habitually to imagine such efforts to be most appropriate. We come to think of the sick, the afflicted and the dying, as those to whom the offers of the Gospel are best fitted; and the next step is to think of them as not fitted for the healthy and the prosperous, who have length of days in prospect. We come to speak of the *consolations* of religion, as if it were only for the evil days; and because it glories in administering peace to those for whom there is no other peace, in drying the tears of the mourner, and in giving victory to the dying believer, we insult it by leaving it, in our thoughts, no other dominion but the house of mourning, the chamber of sickness and the bed of death.

Of course, the occasion which is thus afforded, receives a tenfold strength from the natural indisposition to any serious effort in religion. Man loves the delusion, even while he knows it to be a delusion, which permits him to be quiet, and live to himself alone. Hint to him that piety is the special grace and comfort of the evil day, and till the evil day he rejoices to postpone all study of piety. I recollect an incident mentioned by a missionary in New Holland, in which human nature spoke out its simple reluctance to work out its salvation. The natives of that country were the very lowest of barbarians, without the least subtlety of mind, or skill in reasoning. One of them was told by the missionary, of eternity, of the judgment, of the joys of heaven, and of the damnation of the wicked. The strong and stupid savage heard him, and answered plainly, "I am young and lusty; many years will come before that day; I will wait." There it is; the whole foundation of the postponement of our highest and only necessary business. The natural heart wishes to put it off, as long as it dares; and thus it chooses to represent it as the resource of declining and decaying life; and chooses not, before the evil day, to remember its Creator.

But, besides this direct consequence that religion is postponed, in entire accordance with the wishes of the carnal mind, a more indirect influence is also produced, tending towards its entire neglect. Religion is made gloomy. It is associated with those sorrowful scenes, which none can prefer to contemplate. It comes always to the mind, in the severe and solemn garb of mourning. In the earlier years of life, the taste for all which is joyous is the natural operation of health, and carelessness, and innocence, and inexperience. The grave is not to childhood, what it is to maturity. It is a thought which too often banishes from the young eye its accustomed mirth, without bringing the image of serene and holy peace. If, then, religion be habitually represented as a mere preparation for death, such minds must somewhat avoid the contemplation. It will not be a favorite subject; when they speak of it, a solemn silence will follow; the face will take a sad and rigid aspect; they may perhaps flee to it in affliction; but they will probably shun it in prosperity. So, alas! it is; and, far too generally, the young and the light-hearted, even those who are best disposed, even those who might much more easily take and bear the easy yoke of Christ, than such as are older and more hardened, even these are led to satisfy themselves with respecting religion as the comfort which, when they shall have lived longer and suffered more, they may seek for themselves, rather than as the light and employment and joy of all their years.

Let us now listen to the counsel of inspiration, "Remember thy Creator while the evil days come not;" and let us be satisfied that these modes of viewing the Gospel as simply adapted to the evil days, are delusive and wrong, and most dangerous. It is not for any of us to say that the Gospel cannot save those who flee to its promises for succor in the season of their trouble. Thank God, it can; and blessed be his holy name that such multitudes, turning to him in their affliction, have owned with overflowing hearts that it has been good for them that they have been afflicted. Nevertheless, we must say that neither is affliction, of any kind, the best season for learning to serve God; nor is it a particularly appropriate season for serving him; nor is it a season when he can be served as he has commanded. They who seek God then, do not seek him in that way in which he has specially promised that he will be found; a promise specially given to those who seek him early. It is not the time for doing the work which is laid upon a Christian. They embrace religion under great disadvantage. They embrace it when they have reason to expect from it less of enjoyment and confidence. They embrace it when, if they are indeed sincere, they must have great pain that they have refused to embrace it before. They embrace it when it is absolutely impossible for them to fulfil some of its chief duties, or to experience some of its best delights. They embrace it when, except through some extraordinary grace and fruit, they must have less of peace on earth, and of recompense in heaven.

This is a strong statement, and is meant to be such; for, we can hardly speak with too much strength, if we might thus hope to overcome this ungrateful, absurd, and dreadful determination to give to God only the last and the least, only what we positively cannot as well as dare not withhold. But I would especially urge the command to remember the Creator while the evil days come not, because then only can we serve him as we ought. What is the nature and office of religion? Is it merely to save a sinner from punishment? Is it merely that he may be pardoned? No; for we were made to glorify God with our body and our spirit, which are his. No; for the Son of God has redeemed us with his most precious blood, that he might purify unto himself a peculiar people, zealous of good works. No; for the Lord has given us precious talents, to "occupy till he come;" and has assured us that "he will render unto every man according as his works shall be." The day of judgment is too much omitted from our regard. According to the deeds done in the body, must be the recompense; and we must either go away into everlasting punishment, or into life eternal, according as we have done the deeds of the righteous or of the wicked. When must these deeds be done? In the years of life, not commonly in the hours of death, or the mere days of sorrow. What are our talents? Health, and youthful vigor, and the clear powers of the mind, are almost the first. So far as it is the work of religion to do the will of God, and "by patient continuance in well-doing to seek for glory, honor and immortality," so far, you perceive that it must be accomplished "while the evil days come not, nor the years draw nigh, in which you shall say, I have no pleasure in them." It is a fearful thing to postpone all till the last moment; to do it deliberately; and then to come to Christ at length with a repentance which we dare not trust; even if then we have any longer any disposition to come, and are not shut up in utter hardness of heart.

The word of God appeals to nobler motives; and with such an appeal would we now close. Come to the vineyard of the Lord, and work while the day lasteth; and when the shadows of evening gather, he will give your reward. Arise and follow the blessed Jesus, whose yoke is easy, and whose burden is light; and who will give rest unto your souls. Give up your hearts to the gracious Father, who knoweth what need ye have of all things, and will take care of your happiness; without whom not a sparrow falls to the ground, and in whose sight ye are of more value than many sparrows. Love him who has purchased you with so rich a ransom, and live to him who died for you, and rose again; it is all which your gratitude can offer. Come, and be fellow-workers with God, and with angels, and with all the good, past, present and to come, in the glorious work of bringing innumerable souls to happiness and glory. Take to you the armor of God, and shrink not from this warfare against principalities and powers, in which you must be either with or against the blessed Redeemer. All this is to be done "while the evil days come not, nor the years draw nigh, in which you shall say, that you have no pleasure in them." Oh, if you would reach the kingdom of heaven at last, and then would look back with joy upon a path of fruitful service and of peace, leave not the religion of the Gospel to be only your resource in adversity. When the evil days come, let them find you, knowing, by long experience, whom you have believed, and assured that he will keep that which you have committed unto him, through every day, of tempest or of sunshine, till the triumphant end.

SERMON XIX.

REMAINDER OF LIFE.

St. James, iv. 15.

"IF THE LORD WILL, WE SHALL LIVE, AND DO THIS OR THAT."

EVERY man is the possessor of a life, as of any other blessing within his power of employment. He will seem to himself to hold it as to himself he seems to hold all the others, whether without a cause beyond his own nature, or through some accidental allotment, or from his Supreme Creator and Governor. If he forget the Lord of all, he may still, taught by a constant and sad experience, forbear to speak of the future, except with the express or implied condition, that his life be not shortened. But if he be at once irreligious, and eager or thoughtless, he will probably disregard all possible contingencies, and say, with those whom the Apostle addressed, "to-day, or to-morrow, we will go into such a city, and continue there a year, and buy and sell, and get gain." St. James reproves such confidence in so frail a thing as our mortal life, and such neglect of the Providence of God. He gives, in the text, the form, which, whether incorporated into our customary speech, or silently and reverently intimated by our evident sense of the uncertainty of all events, shall yet denote the habitual attitude of our minds, waiting upon the hand of the Lord, and feeling that we are pilgrims here.

Still, life is, even in that form of words, our possession: only it is held from God, and held by the tenure of his will alone. So long as he gives it, so long it is ours; and as such it must be regarded and employed. The mind can never limit its view to the present moment: while it attempts it, that moment is passed. It never was designed, that, because we cannot know that another day will be allowed us, we should have no scheme or purpose for the time to come. Any effort so to live would issue in a most criminal waste of our best earthly treasures. The scriptural injunction, on the contrary, expressly permits that, when we have acknowledged the entire dependence of all upon the good pleasure of our God, we should think, wish and determine, for the days which, whether they be more or fewer, are our own. "If the

Lord will," we ought to say; and then we may and should add, "we shall live, and do this or that." For, none are called to live without hopes or fears or ends.

Let me beseech you, then, to contemplate, the first great fact of our knowledge; the fact that we live, and shall live, here upon earth. If the Lord will, we shall rise with the light of to-morrow; and accordingly we prepare ourselves for its duties, and retire to rest, which is a part of the preparation. If the Lord will, we shall live to complete various enterprises, to gather in harvests, nay, to train up families; and it is right to follow, in our actions, the probability which, as reasoning beings, we cannot despise. We must leave no weighty interests at the hazard of a probability, if it may be rendered certain; but we must do many things for the sake of that which can be no more than probable, though it rise to the utmost height of such evidence.

A period of time, be it what it may, is the allotted inheritance of every one of us. The journey has soon its end; but the way must be trodden till then. To sever the thread of life, by violence, is made by the law of God the chief of crimes, when it is done in malice; as it is the very highest prerogative of human authority, when it is done in the administration of justice, and the very last resort of necessity, when it is done in defence. Self-murder is esteemed a deed which could not well be wrought, till after the loss, either of soundness of mind, or else of the conscious conviction of accountability to God; because it is so plainly an attempt to usurp that power which he has reserved to himself, and to reject the ends for which he has given us existence. For the same cause, if a person could be imagined, who, through bodily or mental weakness, should be so impressed with the constant expectation of death, as to accomplish nothing except that which the dying would have a heart to perform, it would be only his infirmity which would exempt his negligence from the charge of guilt. All would mourn that the bounties of Providence were so abused, and its purposes so disappointed. It is a kind of suicide to treat life as if it were worthless.

Believe, then, that you are to live, while you remember that it may be but for a very short season; a season rapidly fleeting onward. It passes not, however, too rapidly to be clearly seen and grasped, as if with the hand, and examined with a steady eye. The young person, who begins a course of instruction, which must occupy a fixed period; the mariner who sets out on a long voyage; the man who holds an office, or hires an abode, for a term of years; is more uncertain of its completion than of his life; for, besides his death, other events, also, may break his plan in the midst; and yet, it is his wisdom to survey the whole period from its beginning; and to devise, arrange and resolve, for such an use of the time as shall most enlarge his profit. So let each of you anticipate that portion of life, which is yet untrodden. Wherever you may stand, whether just leaving the boundaries of childhood, or on the verge of mature manhood, or at the point where the first infirmities of age are felt, or even beyond, where the way declines steadfastly towards the tomb, yet make it to yourselves a real and distinct truth, that you possess a portion of time, which is still to come, and which you are bound to appropriate in accordance with the will of its Sovereign Giver.

This first and simplest truth is, notwithstanding, a wonder which baffles all our inquiries. Of all the mysterious marvels which man has ever known, or believed, or imagined, can any be more mysterious, than his own life? The origin of its existence; the union of the body and the soul; the partial and temporary relaxation of their union at various times; their strange influence on each other; the connection between himself and his fellow-beings; the presence of divine power with him and in him; the freedom which he feels, the dependence which he cannot but discern; the manner in which his senses at once enable him to know so much, and prevent his knowledge of so much more; his position towards other creatures of God, whom he cannot see; his ability to think of objects infinite or almost infinite, which his thoughts can never half embrace, so that, placed on this globe, he can look out into boundless space, and placed here during a few of its revolutions, can look out into eternity; how amazing and incomprehensible is all! To pause and wonder may indeed seem to avail little; yet it is profitable to feel and say with the Psalmist, "I am fearfully and wonderfully made: marvellous are thy works, and that my soul knoweth right well." For, he who regards his very being as a gift so far surpassing his understanding, is led by that conviction of weakness to remember habitually its Author; to feel that it may have, and has, other purposes than those of this world; and to lay a firm hold upon that chain which joins the visible to the invisible, life to death, to judgment, and to the retribution of hell and heaven.

The fact, the wonder, which we thus contemplate, must be contemplated next as a blessing.

A few years more are ours upon earth; and they are given, not in wrath, but in love. Not on this side of the grave should a mortal cease to bless the Father of all mercies for creation and preservation. It is a duty to enjoy the fountains of pure, blameless and worthy pleasure which he has commanded to flow along both sides of the straight and narrow way of righteousness. When once the hope of divine peace prevails in the heart, it is met by a delicate fear which the world will hardly comprehend; the fear lest the blessings of this life, now tasted first in all their sweetness, should themselves be made the instruments of beguiling it too far. The sinner is conscious of the guilt of those sinful enjoyments which he strives to create for himself; but he apprehends not, like the Christian, the enjoyment which life itself, the more in proportion as it is pure, can be and can impart, without deviation or excess; enjoyment, which is to that of the sinner, what the cool rivulet, touching the lip of the traveller, is to the fiery cup of inebriation; what the playful mirth of a domestic circle is to the heated revelry of a company of gamesters. So true it is, that religion "adds a fresh interest to every thing worth knowing, and a fresh grace to every thing worth doing." I am aware, indeed, that for one who calmly looks across these years, and steadfastly feels himself immortal, it can be but very little, though his lot upon earth should seem to be only sorrow. What is the rivulet that refreshes the traveller, if the lights of his home are already in view? What is the circle of domestic quiet, when the lasting safety, usefulness and peace of all, calls forth the father and the husband to strenuous, self-denying toil? But there are seasons, too, for repose; and toil also has its alacrity, and the journey has its delight; the more as the step draws near to the fair walls which we seek; the more as the pleasant breezes of evening waft the dear sounds of home. We are bound to accept the period which is still before us, whatever griefs it may bring, and however our errors may change its character, as yet a gracious gift of paternal love; the more, that it is given to be the road to heaven.

Yet life must also be contemplated as a season of affliction. No prophetic inspiration is needed, to tell the common sorrows which must come, in proportion as the period is prolonged. Every bridal union must be severed; the longer life of the survivor is only on the condition of the added grief. Every parent and child must be separated: the only doubt concerns the proportion, not the certainty, of mutual suffering. He who dies young must go to the grave amidst the warmest tears: he who is taken in the middle of his days must leave a weight of peculiar care to those who would have found dependence on his arm; he who accomplishes the full age of man must be lonely and infirm, the relic of past times, missing the companions who were his chief solace and joy. It is our wisdom and our happiness, not to shrink from this view, but to seek to be ready for the evil day, which cannot be very far distant.

A thoughtful mind, indeed, accustomed to the uncertainties of all events, is reminded of that day by the very exemption which may have been long granted by a gracious Providence. If you are a member of a family, which, by the goodness of God, has been preserved without a breach much longer than those by which it is surrounded, suffer not yourselves to be lulled into a dream that this peace will be continued: the time must be approaching, and the common mode of reflection would countenance the thought that you ought to anticipate it, even more than others. "Shall we receive good at the hand of God, and shall we not receive evil?" If our portion till now has seemed to be of good alone, must not the ills which descend on all, be anticipated as hastening on, with sure though silent feet? Were they, indeed, but thus expected; would we but arm ourselves in prosperity as in tribulation we would desire to be armed, they might be changed into blessings. The remembrance of uninterrupted and undefiled friendship would be grateful, even when that friendship had been checked in its intercourse by death. The pious use of joys would confirm the cheerful hope of their renewal at the end. As each earthly gift, with which we must part, was humbly yielded up, it would be only that the soul might turn with more tried and purified love, to its God and Saviour, and receive in return, now in hope and at last in felicity, far more than it had surrendered.

The life which is before us, whatever be its duration, is the time within which our preparation for the bliss of the servants of God must be accomplished, if ever. Some of you, are doubtless walking even now in an opposite way. The work which was given you to do is not begun; and the period that remains may be much less than that which has been lost. Others are surely conscious that they earnestly desire, above all things, the crown of him that endureth and overcometh; but so much the more gladly do they accept the exhortation which bids them gird up the loins of their minds, be sober, and watch unto the end. Here is the infinite worth of human life; and here, therefore, must we fix our firmest stand, and strive to send forth our voice with most awakening energy. As vast as is the distance between that highest heaven to which a child of man shall ever ascend and that deepest depth of woe in which human guilt shall ever groan; as vast as is the immensity of duration over which no thought can stretch its wing; as vast as are the capabilities, which, planted by the Creator in the immortal spirit, wait to develop themselves in the beams of his love through all eternity; so vast are the dignity and the value of that short space which thou must tread, before thou go hence and be no more seen. Within that space, the soul may be destroyed; within it, the soul may be saved. Within that space he who now hears and fears, because he knows that he is far from God, may become an heir of glory; within it, he who now exults with vain, unfounded confidence, may become a castaway. Within that space, such deeds of love may be done, as shall be to many souls that shall come after, seeds of eternal life and peace; within it, there is time enough to corrupt, by example, by negligence, by persuasion, or by the manifold evils that flow from evil deeds, multitudes who may lift up their reproaching and condemning cry in the regions of despair. Within that space, the heart may become the pure temple of God, and, being delivered from all the unclean passions by which it had been haunted, may come to reflect from its surface the image of angelic loveliness; within it, the same heart may so surrender itself to the dominion of ungodliness, that at length it shall cling to the chains of Satan, and be, like him, a tempter, wherever it can find resemblance to a Paradise, till it lies down in shame and everlasting burnings. The longest life which may yet remain to any of us is not too long, the shortest is, doubtless, not too short, to prepare us for a place in heaven. But the view of our life as the time of probation divides itself, when we speak of its length; has thus a twofold character; and deserves, in each, our most faithful contemplation.

It cannot be known to any man, but it may possibly be fixed in the purpose of God, that some careless hearer of these words may have in reserve only a few days upon earth. Every person who dies has listened to some one sermon as the last: nothing would be less surprising than that this should be the last to some one of its hearers. If it were thus, and that very person, blind to the peculiar happiness of his own escape, should yet be led to-day to consider the solemnity of his condition as a living mortal, embarked for an eternal voyage, and should call on God from the midst of his helplessness, and come, with an earnest heart, to Him who is mighty to save, and yield himself up to be his disciple, certainly though his days, while he knew it not, were so numbered that they could not be measured by weeks, there would yet be joy in heaven, for his sake, and a mansion made ready for him with the Lord. There is no need to fear that the assertion of this truth, in all its glory, will be more exposed than that of other Christian doctrines, to presumptuous abuse. While the history of the malefactor who died with our Lord Jesus remains in the narrative of St. Luke, a history that goes straight home to every heart, a history which Providence appointed to be precisely so arranged that it should most unequivocally declare the acceptance of penitence, late but true; it would be exceeding presumption to doubt that the shortest life may be sufficient.

But it is probable, also, that the lives of most who hear me will be extended to months and years. If, then, each of them could be secure that such would be his lot; and if it were a thing of no moment whether his sins were more or less numerous and heinous, so that he were but safe in the end; and if the will of God were not to be admitted into his thoughts; and if punishment were to be regarded as only an unhappy accident, to be averted by a certain method; and if the influence of each of us over others were not worthy of mention; and if our Maker had no task for us to do in his service on earth; and if the tendency of all habits were not towards increased strength; and if the Holy Spirit could not withdraw, nor the heart become hardened; and if there were no sin unto death; many, who are wise in their generation, might hold it wise to secure this world at present, and might deem a long life more than sufficient to prepare them for that which shall come after. But were you, my brethren, admitted to see, in its reality, one year of rebellion against God, with all its guilt, its misery, its danger, its results, as it is bound to that cause which it serves, you would probably pause no longer. You would start from your security, and exclaim, that a moment is too much to be subtracted from the work of rescue, out of such peril and such woe.

Once more, then, we recur, after these successive views of our remaining life, to our first station. "If the Lord will," each one of us has a right to say, "I shall live, and do this or that." Every man who does not design to be the sport of every wind of good or evil, must be inwardly saying this in the general habit of his thoughts and actions. Every man has some scheme of life, whatever it be; even the most idle must build one on the necessities of the hour, one extending no further than these; while the worldly and prudent have a plan that embraces all their existence here, and the believer in Christ has framed his own from counsels that originated above, and reach beyond, the scenes which they now govern. What is it that if the Lord will, and you live, you will do? What shall be the history of the time which is still yours?

It is your part, my brethren, to make that history; but it will be recorded on high, and it will be read hereafter. The life of each is, indeed, a history of far more weight than that of any nation, as these are viewed by eyes that cannot look beyond this visible world. It is easy to anticipate the time when, while it is read or remembered, all other reflections will be subordinate to one, all other relations to that which links it to the everlasting realm of righteousness or of death. Oh, may its purport be then like this! "He saw the worth of the treasure which he held within his grasp. He determined that, through the grace of God, the life which was given to prepare him, if he would, for heaven, should not fail of its design. He prayed that, whatever should be its other employments, this might be the chief; that, whatever should be its joys, they might receive no added glow from the charms of sinful pleasure; that, whatever might be its sorrows, they might be the discipline of his soul, and might issue at last in peace; and that, whatever else he might want or possess, God would bestow on him, for Christ's sake, the faith that overcometh the world. He passed firmly by the entrance of each successive path of temptation, and pressed on, turning neither to the right hand nor to the left; or, when he erred, and was graciously recalled, returning with a meek and steadfast, though an humbled spirit. He strove to make it his meat and drink to do, in his place, the will of his heavenly Father. He lived no longer for himself alone, but for his fellow-men, for generations to come, for the cause of truth and love, for God and heaven; and, having finished his course, behold him with the just made perfect! Many of us, my brethren, will surely say, 'If the Lord will, we shall live, and do this!'"

THE END.

III.

THE BOY TRAINED TO BE A CLERGYMAN. By the Rev. J. N. Norton. Second edition enlarged, price 37 cts.

"This little book gives the trials and experiences of a boy's life through college, his preservation by the great purpose of his life,—his good influence on his companions. Altogether it is a most pleasing and instructive book."

IV.

PRACTICAL RELIGION. Exemplified by Letters and Passages from the Life of the late Rev. Robert Anderson. By the Hon. Mrs. Anderson. 75 cents.

V.

THE STAR OF THE WISE MEN. Being a Commentary of the second chapter of St. Matthew. By Richard Chenevix Trench, B. D. 37 cents.

VI.

HARDWICK'S HISTORY OF THE XXXIX ARTICLES OF THE CHURCH OF ENGLAND. 8vo., $1 75.

VII.

TRENCH'S HULSEAN LECTURES. One volume, 12mo., 75 cents.

VIII.

LAST ENEMY CONQUERING AND CONQUERED. By Bishop Burgess. 12mo. 75 cents.

IX.

THE PRIVATE PRAYER BOOK. Being a Collection of Devotions for Daily and Hourly use. Compiled from Holy Scriptures and Godly Writings. By Rev. William H. Odenheimer. 50 cents.

X.

HYMNS FOR LITTLE CHILDREN. By the Author of the "Lord of the Forest," "Verses for Holy Seasons," &c.

XI.

FIRST PRINCIPLES OF THE DOCTRINE OF CHRIST. By M. P. Parks, of Trinity Church, New York. 50 cents.

www.ingramcontent.com/pod-product-compliance
Lightning Source LLC
LaVergne TN
LVHW020235110826
845151LV00003B/928